Living Your Life According to Connecting the Dots by Numbers

Living Your Life According to Connecting the Dots by Numbers

By

R.A Feller

About the Book

Faith gives way to praise opening the door to eternity. This allows us to experience the order of life in a time base out of order world. Where there is order there's an absolute and fellowship with Jesus from His world, the King and giver of life. Things are not always what they appear to be. Are we following projected images on our minds or reality? To find meaning one has to search out answers.

As Joseph stored grain for seven years, God has blessed me by storing up understanding for the times of famine in every day life.

Living Your Live According to Connecting the Dots by Number was written for me to help me understand who I am and what God's plan is for my life. Writing this book restored sanity to my life by pushing out the dark lies of misperceptions and packing my mind with the light of God's truth in its place. Jesus navigates, I trust and follow. Now it is my desire to share my vision and help others to grow in His body (Love + Truth = Light), that they may face life's journey and deal with problems with a close relationship with God to see them through as he does me.

My Testimony

In my 39 years of life I have tasted death and life enough to know the difference between them. These are my scars, healed by God's glory in the blood of Jesus Christ. I was raised a Jew steeped in misperception, spiritually dead with no bonding love with my parents and abusive babysitters, who would not allow me to express myself. Sometimes I got hit, most of the time neglected and due to unhealthy boundaries, being extremely needy, I became the neighborhood scapegoat becoming the butt end of a joke along with beatings which lead me to writing graffiti and belonging to street gangs, where I got acceptance. I became a graffiti king on the New York City Subway System, and had many near-death experiences. As a shoplifter with no conscience I stole thousands of dollars worth of spray paint and vandalized where I pleased, in underground train yards, tunnels and elevated yards. This was an escape, I acted out criminally letting my emotions drive me from my childhood pain which included a workaholic father, an incestuous atmosphere with my mother and a non-bonding love, goal-orientated upbringing which caused me to have a survivor mentality. I sold drugs. Once two men tried to overpower me in a stairwell. One had a choke hold on me so I bit him in the arm then knocked him down the stairs, the other took to flight. Soon after becoming sexually addicted, having no honor, I became a male prostitute and later committed adultery. After this my flesh ruled me, even murder, an abortion did not phase me. Sex was on my mind all of the time and I could have it when I wanted, along with money and drugs, only I could not see the emptiness of them. Soon after I was talked to, although I didn't know it at the time, by one of the boys who used to beat me up on my block. He gradually introduced me to Jesus Christ who opened my eyes little by little and into a relationship with Him.

Before this I met a girl in a bar who went to prayer meetings and lived like the devil. I went along to Catholic church and although the people were nice it was just religion not Jesus, like my old synagogue. This Jewish girl took an interest in me, helped me with school work and encouraged me to get my driver's license. At the age of 22 I finished college and soon after married the girl who seemed to care about me. She was pretty and her dad was rich.

Ever since high school I'd been deeply involved in the film and video industry. After a total of 10 years, over 200 commercials, 3 feature films, a number of industrial productions as well as my own cable TV shows. Attending Christ-centered churches, God got my attention and called me out. My wife was finishing in her Ph.D. in psychology, my career was slow starting. My wife became pregnant. It was after the birth of our first daughter that my wife stopped school. I felt money pressures, also I could no longer work with a clear conscience on most of my shoots. Work became idolatry. God was not being glorified and the door to this world became closed. I became a school teacher at Clinton High School in the Bronx teaching ESL to new students from other countries. At this time God spoke to me about idols which were dear to my heart and not his.

Anything I bought with blood money through illegal means, along with my scripts, records, poetry (I'm published by American Collegian poets, with honors), hobbies, and material possessions, all turned to death. I destroyed thousands of dollars of material possessions threw away blood money, camera equipment, including my writings, which were dear to me, but they were all in the way of my relationship with Christ Jesus the self had to die. I started to minister in the streets and gained experience in the spiritual world. Healings and watching people get filled with the spirit of Christ as I shared with them from God's word were all pay for the course. Christ had become apart of my life and I His. My wife had me commit myself to a mental hospital, according to her experience as almost a Ph.D. in psychology, as she was my wife. I laid down my life and entered in. I was observed and put on medication, reassured the medicine wouldn't affect our relationship.

My spiritual writing was deemed as insane. Discouraged from writing any further for seven years I did not pick up a pen to creative writing either; I would not let 'self' talk. Until one day I saw my three children fighting, all at once I saw the truth of the situation and wrote it down as a children's story. Then more stories came. Writing out what I saw in spiritual visions. No longer out of imagination, soon after I realized writing what I see was not mine but given to me. Later I came across Psalm 45:1, a bible verse which spoke of having the pen of the 'ready writer' and saw this is where my writing is coming from, divine inspiration, this confirmed I was sane. I'm in awe the way God uses people without them even being aware of it most of the time. After praying about it for sometime I left teaching and went to work for my father-in-law where currently I am manager/mechanic in a packing plant walking before the Lord with a clear conscience. My wife wants out of our marriage, which is where things are now, but Christ has prepared a place for me in the midst of the pain. We've been separated a year now and I've found a place in Christ where he has all my fondest affections. I'm content and my relationship with Jesus Christ has made the difference.

Forward

We're on a journey, one thread of truth line woven in at a time. The way is built for our direction, a guide for the way. Peter 5:10, but may the God of all grace, who called us to His eternal glory by Jesus Christ, after you have suffered a while, perfect, establish, strengthen, and settle you. All else is desolation; a land of lost circles where dogs chase their tales in blind sight.

People don't see where spiritual life comes from. This is why they break spiritual laws and miss life. Relationships are apart of these laws as they build and grow they produce, 'when mature', fruit for life and death. To get to know another person intimately you need to spend a great deal of time with them. We need time alone with Christ, in His spirit, twenty four hours a day in the face of our surroundings, friendly or hostile to walk, talk, dine and sleep with Jesus "for He's packed with life." Ever before our face to learn of Him and see Him as we pass through time, to draw from Him. I have someone in me who wants to come out. Be consciously aware, by God's grace, we're possessed by God to experience His grace when we speak believing in, on and through Jesus Christ.

The scenery is changing and people too, but Christ remains the same. The Holy Spirit operates by empowering us to reflect the character of the living God. Following Jesus means eternal life but death to our 'self,' an end to our ways, yet I follow cause I've tasted life. I know sanctification is a process and beyond the pains of death to the flesh is His eternal life. As He leads me gently on, through this world below, my mind is His continually; He's all I'll ever want to know.

In breaking through the dark flow that's contrary to His light, my soul lives with His spirit leaving the past behind as my desire is to experience everything renewed. Joy in the face of adversity as each new mystery is revealed. We bow not to seek our own, but to let out the life of Christ, that it may be made known in the open face of all. That He may be glorified and bless all by the spirit of His presence. I say with John, Oh that I may decrease that He may increase all the more. When I made the decisions for me, the cords of my life which seemed so right were tied to an anchor pulling me steadily downward, deeper into darkened depths. Jesus liberated me breaking cords, one strand at a time, gradually to lighten my load till the weight was all gone. I'm rising from death unto life through an open door. Jesus by the way He lives His life is a sample from the eternal world. When reviled he reviled not, darkness could not get in to exist with the light. Jesus' 'focus,' a sample drink to do the Father's will of the ocean of God. For us to see God is good and test to gain understanding as we enter into a relationship with Him, making what is invisible visible. Christ paid it all and paved the way for us, all we're to do is ask Him and Jesus accepts us as part of His eternal life family.

As the surface of the waters are still, only then can it reflect the sun brilliantly, and we the image of Christ the end of our journey. Choppy waters that are wind-driven fragment the rays of the sun and leave us feeling dull, without understanding the true vision for the direction we're to go. Once we see the son through the shadowy unreality's of time, press in without taking Him for granted, then we'll find our mark, the high calling, and know the direction we must take. To learn to discern what we're following for life makes a difference. There are principles of closing the windows to keep in what gives life and out what does not. This book gradually opens the door to the way we view reality. To focus on where the eternal pierces the temporal, as we cry out, "Be my all in all," and examine if we're to continue on the path following Christ and how we're changed as we remain content in experiencing God's love.

Chapter Summary

Chpt -1- <u>Connecting the Dots</u>
This chapter captures, in rapid succession, the formation from instability, to a stable identity with a Christ-centered reality as an end product.

Chpt -2- <u>Dotted Picture Interaction</u>
Once having stability with a Christ-center what takes place as we interact with others, in the unseen realm? There's competition for our actions and spoken words which will yield power for creation to produce spiritual life or death. This chapter opens the door to unseen battles to make one aware to better prepare for the struggle of everyday life, putting on Christ.

Chpt -3- <u>Space Survival In Unreality</u>
This chapter deals with the eternal reality of Love + Truth = Light finding its way through the unreality of Lies + Hate = Darkness in Time. The shift which brings clarity to perceptual balance also examines its source of life.

Chpt -4- <u>God Will Only Be In Control If You Let Him</u>
God can only work with someone who admits to living in darkness and needs His help to get out of this condition. We need to ask to be taught how to survive in a relative world. To escape the devil's tactics of deception which lead to death we must call on God in time of need and He'll be there to set us free.

Chpt -5- <u>Transformation</u>
This chapter explains how one gets transformed from a time-based past into an eternal life-giving future. How faith changes our perception through greater understanding of conflict in everyday life. We learn to make choices of order which include calling on God, to keep us from chaos.

Chpt -6- <u>Space Extension</u>

The more life is extended from a space and interacts with others the more life we will cultivate. This process affects our heritage one fiber at a time, then chain reaction confrontation, what is left will enhance or detract from who we are.

Chpt -7- <u>How Much Are We Worth In the Kingdom of Light?</u>
<u>(God's Kingdom)</u>

Every time the darkness of time is pushed out, we increase in value. Our Christ-given worth luminates us as we are hammered out into greater value with every new experience. We have eternal worth though darkness would try to get us to forget our past growth and lose sight of this. We live for ever our value never ends, as we're shaped as Kings on our way from glory to glory staying true in His righteousness, we reign with Christ.

Chpt -8- <u>Feelings</u>

How am I loving and honest with myself and others? How do I confront the truth of others in situations that arise without giving myself away? These questions are related to the way we think, our thoughts, and emote our emotions. This chapter looks at the need to bring them together to make the best choices for ourselves due to the damage which can occur in the dark recesses of timebase unreality, apart from God's domain.

Chpt -9- <u>The Last Dot</u>

This chapter looks at the original relationship God had with Adam and how his poor choice to disobey God, going against the Holy Spirit, still affects us today. We were never created to be alone and as the damage is repaired through Christ, we regain our understanding of the fellowship with God, without which we'd starve for lack of life.

Chpt -10- <u>Prayers, Poems and Visions Through Growth</u>

During the time this book was under construction many poems and prayers came forth as a part of my vision. I share them with you that you may be encouraged as well.

Chpt -11- <u>In the Flow</u>
Just as we learn to speak a language we must learn to speak the language of the Holy Spirit. We must sense where our words begin and end. Just as we've fingertips with the sense of touch, our body can become sensitive to the Holy Spirit. <u>In the Flow</u> contains a collection of writings which encounter and learn some of the movings of the Holy Spirit.

Chpt -12- <u>Under Attack</u>
Beware of serpents that lay wait in others in shadowy places, who stray from the light of God, rejecting His word and Spirit, even though they profess to know Him. This chapter gives a strong offensive position to strengthen us against the attacks of the devil by making us fully aware of the Eternal as reality.

Chpt -13- <u>Treasure Chest</u>
"....they are trained to look in a temporal direction which makes it difficult for them to experience the eternal."
Choice verses and a collection of individual thoughts compiled prayerfully. Although written over the course of a year this chapter comes together as one cohesive unit.

Chpt -14- <u>The Gift</u>
This chapter examines the provisions God has for us in every day life as He wants us to know and experience them. This is a look into understanding how God's infrastructure meets our needs, lifts us, and bonds us into relationships which are eternally secure.

Chpt -15- <u>Diagrams</u>
These diagrams are geared towards making the abstract more concrete for greater understanding. A look behind the scenes for greater comprehension of how God works in our lives.

Chpt -16- <u>Insights</u>
Over 400 insights, I've gained through the vision of my book, which helped to stabilize my relationship with the Lord

Jesus Christ yielding to deeper life, not to settle for anything less than what God has for me.

Chpt -17- <u>Walking With Jesus In His Service</u>

Some of many miracles as the Spirit of Jesus flow through me and breathe life to many others. Healings, salvation and the pulling down of strong holds all take place in this work.

Connecting the Dots

"In the beginning God created the heavens and the earth and the earth was without form (such as I), and void; and darkness was upon the face of the deep." I had no vision to find my way. "And the spirit of God moved upon the face of the waters." My tears stepped aside. "And God said, 'let there be light': and there was light." The clouds of darkness became parted in my mind. I'd wept to my God and now He was here. From the midst of my suffering... and now He was here! "And God saw the light, that it was good: and God divided the light from the darkness." My heart rose up to receive the embrace of His love. I was lifted up to higher ground, a higher place. Where death can no longer sting. I'd been grafted in to understand, direction to follow, I'd received my sight. Out from the chamber of death did I fly away with the Lord, to be captive no more. Love lifted me. If we have a healthy complete picture of what love is, then we're not going to go where love is not. If we just have one or a few pieces of love, or even as clueless as I was as to what it is, then we're going to get into trouble. Whether things are going great or not so good you'll grow and understand why as you join me on my dot-connecting journey and slowly enter a healthy relationship reality.

As I find my way through space and time I encounter dots, which I've discovered to be beads of truth. The more dots I find, the more I can stop guessing who I am, without any help or lack of understanding. I watch how people respond to my behavior. I've become the joke of conversation which I overhear in bits and pieces and the sad part about it is, I laugh along with them, not realizing my friends are abusive enemies. How blind we can be when we run from our pain unaware that it's there. I tried to enter into friendships without understanding what love is and got pain in its place, thinking it was love.

Then I discovered a dot one day when someone treated me especially well worthwhile. The fact that someone loved me helped me to find Dot #1: VALIDATED. In the midst of all the commotion and unrest, warped perceptions and walk through empty spaces watching life pass me by, I could now hug myself and know I was loved by GOD yet I was still unable to see my great value. There just wasn't enough of me together, but I tasted, God is good, my relationship with Him had begun as did my journey to love.

All of a sudden, I started, very gradually, to see things differently. I could be contained in a space from which I could start to grow, and although very limited, I could start to focus in the midst of all the turmoil that would sweep over me in distorted perceptions. Yes I discovered Dot #2: I HAVE MY OWN SPACE and began to become aware what wasn't love in it.

Now all those punks who trashed me would have to step aside, cause I wasn't running away from the abuse to come back and get more. I walked away and found other friends who accepted me for who I was, only what I didn't know was it was a bad crowd and history was soon to repeat itself. Although my space was growing I lacked the wisdom to manage new friendships, my friends were now con artists who used me for what they could get out of me. I'd be sweet-talked into trusting them and then they would steal things from me: my sister's bicycle, a tape recorder, cash, jewelry, etc. Whenever my back was turned something would be gone. I would try to deny it, hoping things would turn up, then I'd have to face it and once again I was left victimized. I discovered my judgment was bad and Dot #3: BALANCE. In balance, I realized that most of my perceptions about the world in which I lived were warped. My family, friends, enemies and television, classmates and teachers were from bad to very poor role models. I was drowning, treading in unhealthy thoughts, unfortunately many of them I acted out without realizing the stifling consequences. And once in this off balance soup all other styles of living were out of the picture. I needed stability. Something or someone I could turn to and know my perceptions could trust to be healthy, always the same. Then I met Dot #4: TRUTH CONSTANT. He's all-knowing, has perfect self control, is kind to others and loves

2

everybody earnestly and has eternal balance which is <u>non changing</u>. This is what makes it true. Non changing is something I can build on and trust the bottom won't drop out from under me. I started reading the Bible and found the balance and stability I'd been looking for. I started to grow in my space over a period of several years. However, my perceptions had been warped due to a damaged upbringing of unhealthy love and my Bible interpretations did not allow me to grow to who God intended me to be because of it. Instead I lived in a fraction of my space which is Dot #5: SECTIONED which left me with limitations which needed to be confronted and was my only possibility towards growth. I was comfortable in my old behavior patterns as dysfunctional as they were they were my identity, (my only family), and to confront my limitations would mean I'd have to change, and with this change, confront everything and everybody I'd known in my world. I started to discover in glimpses Jesus Christ alone had to become my focus and with Christ as my head everything will fall into place. I have to rest in Him, "what can I do without Him?" Keep messing up my life! There'd be no turning back to the world I once knew and this extra work load of change was a welcome although overwhelmingly scary thought. Then I discovered Dot #6: REASON & ACTION. I had reason. My life had become worthless, I was living a lie, an unlife and I knew I was worth more according to truth constant Dot #4. I took action. I questioned everything that had control over my life and found I needed to do a better job. Then I discovered standing on my own two feet and Dot #7: CENTERED. I felt my knees buckle at first. I felt like running back to my dysfunction. Intellectually I was here to stay but emotionally I was a mess. The eyes of everyone that was upon me was trying, so it seemed, to tie me down to my old lifestyle. They saw me in a fraction of my own space, living an unlife identity, but thanks to truth constant (after becoming centered), my perception was starting to change. I now had a balanced mind and my emotions noticed and in recovery are making the transition even now as I'm writing to link up my thoughts. As time progresses I'm discovering, from a central vantage point, a desire to know God, and other things

3

such as unresolved conflicts, lies and misperceptions living in my space. As battles arise in my soul these problems come into the light of TRUTH CONSTANT, they must be dealt with swiftly, through prayer, Dot #8 I can talk to God and he can answer me, and not be allowed to grow any larger or they will try to force me back into a section of my space and regain control of my center. Before I committed adultery my, (conscience), thought life was at peace, at rest I had trust with my wife. At age 17, and thinking I was capable of making the best choices for my life, a man propositioned me, money for sex, having no understanding of integrity due to my home atmosphere I accepted this arrangement not knowing that years later it would grow to be uncontrollable and lead to my adultery. He offered to support me financially and give me whatever I wanted: car, apartment, etc. I took a look at what was happening in my mind and came up with off-balanced love. In adultery my thoughts became divided, a secret identity which took away my peace, as it grew larger it stole my life. I became more and more my secret identity. When I stopped the affair as I entered into God's reality and confessed my adultery to my wife I lost my secret identity, my trust from my wife I also lost. Seek ye first the Kingdom of God and His righteousness and all these things shall be added unto you, was on my mind. I had to move, conjure up my best efforts and call it God's will. Before we confess our sins, and God is just and able to forgive us our sins and cleanse us from all unrighteousness. Do we consider, are we in touch with other people's feelings as not to hurt them and in the name of righteousness push them away from God. I grew and had changed however my wife still looked at me as sectioned off with the lie of a secret identity in my space, she didn't see the growth, and wrapped her mind around my secret identity in judgement. I could only live the truth as obedient to God's reality, by His changing power through His grace and not return to the invitation of my old lifestyle, thus breaking the force that would try to regain control of me. However; the same way Abraham did not wait on God's promise, Isaac a son to continue his seed for all generations, through Sarah and begot Ishmael through Hagar a maid, his and his wife's own plan lead to disruption, although in the end God honored his word. Just as my secret identity would have fallen away as I continue to grow in my relationship with God had I waited. I hurt my wife trying to do things on my time table, not allowing God's grace to have its perfect way with me. I disrupted the blessing of my family because of my ignorance in God's ways. Be warned through the experience of my walk, only disruption comes to our space when we do things our own way and not God's.

Dot #9: WHAT'S LIVING IN MY SPACE? First I had to understand who I'm supposed to be. For Truth Constant so loved the world that none should perish but all have eternal life with Him. God, the creator of everything: stars, planets, time, space, flowers, plants, animals, water, etc, created a special plan since the beginning of time for us, He created an eternal door with the use of his son (the word became flesh) who HE would love, cherish and watch grow from infant to man. God would observe his balanced eternal (Door) son be brutally beaten, mocked in all his CONSTANT GLORY, and finally murdered as a spectacle of unmistakable mercy on our behalf while we were yet worthless sinners. So we can be united with Him eternally forever is how valuable I am to Him. As many as touched Him were made whole. It only takes one touch of the reality, God loves and is here now, for us to receive healing, the kind that brings newness of life. I'm valuable and validated, stamped and approved of by God for being me and accepted for who I am by the great I AM. It was truth that opened my eyes. When we take in the things of this world or from religion it will choke our relationship with Christ away. Now I'm learning how to belong to who TRUTH ETERNAL created me to be. Following Truth Constant, I must be patiently watchful and wait to see what is me and what is not. If I'm balanced and have my eyes fully on Jesus, eternal vision, my space should be evenly centered, my limitations (walls or perimeter) should be at peace and rest, as is Jesus the prince of peace. My center, which is woven together is comprised of emotional and logical reasoning, a grid to sense a problem as it arises. If truth is to be gained it causes growth which enlarges our space to prevent deviations in the grid and allow for a maximum flow of life. If a problem is contrary to

TRUTH CONSTANT, it threatens a warp, it distorts as it is a lie, like seeking after lustful relationships or great wealth. If such actions are allowed to fester by the denial of their destructive forces or are allowed to stay as perceived truth, when it's a lie, if not connected to TRUTH CONSTANT through prayer an off balance warp occurs, (disorder). Then this problem if not pushed out of the space will grow over a period of time and if left unchecked will force the central control to shift from TRUTH CONSTANT to false central rule, as in the case of my affair, the person will be sectioned off, imprisoned within their own space, while lies (Demons) rule their center. When my mind wanders into Dot #10, the Time Dimension in which we live and away from Jesus, TRUTH CONSTANT, which leads to Truth Eternal (Eternity), then I find myself off balance by losing sight of who I am. John 17:21...one in us, (the Father and the Son) and become desensitized, void of emotions, and indulgent to misperceptions, (sin is good and not evil). Time is off balance and distorts perceptions. Dot #11, ETERNITY, is balanced as it cuts into the span of time and there is balance in an unbalanced world when Eternity is set in the heart and not imposed on others' spaces. Even if I see others struggling, if I am not invited into their space (and welcomed to stay), the only thing I can continue to do is remember great compassion has Jesus to meet all our needs far beyond what we are able to understand while we grow, so enjoy truth's company and rejoice in His love in the presence of all being salt and light in a stale dark world. Do not do what you do not understand, to do otherwise is off balance and a lie, but understand this to speak the name of Jesus can turn everything around. A relationship with Him and service to Him, both apart of knowing God should be one in the same. Serving God should never take the place of a relationship with the High King or the splendor of His wonder in creation which speaks to us about who He is. God is love, and we love because He first loved us. I love because God first loved me and resting in Him allows us time to bond, to discover what God is eternally like. Col. 3:1 If you have been raised up with Christ, keep seeking the things above, where Christ siteth on the right hand of God. When I was a production coordinator in the film and video industry, I was the producer's right hand man. I needed to anticipate what would come next before I was asked what would come next or I wouldn't be around very long, I was only as good as my last job. As a freelancer one mistake and I wasn't called back. Christ is still at work for us, "As He ever makes intercetion for us", and according to the Bible Jesus keeps His job. We need an eyeful of the glory of Christ in everything we do daily to remain bonded and comprehend God's loving us. Otherwise we start to build a wall and with each brick of doubt we shut God out. However; I believe that, "He who began a good work in us is able to perfect it."

"For so an entrance will be supplied to you abundantly into the everlasting kingdom of our Lord and Savior Jesus Christ."

Dotted Picture Interaction

In a healthy relationship with God through Christ, the ideal is a space centered evenly with a hundred percent truth constant filling it. When this healthy space comes into contact with other spaces, offering truth and love, like a light switch turned on in a dark room, it's going to have an effect on other spaces as when a mother comforts a crying child. Truth constant spaces talk to other spaces one line at a time, in truth, then hold more order, more balance and gradually enlarge other spaces towards a truth center, and then expansion, like blowing up a balloon, starts to take place with a newly born spaces identity as it fills with life. A little truth putting on Christ each day keeps the lie-centered spaces, darkness, from building one lie at a time into another spaces center, to give it a False Identity. A competitive interaction takes place when a truth-centered space is newly born and is around lie-centered peers or, vice versa, lie-centered spaces are around supportive truth-filled spaces as in the case of falling in a good or bad crowd. If a large amount of truth is sectioned off in a lie-centered space and its around both a mostly lie-centered space and a truth-centered space similar competition can take place and may even cause an identity crisis. All contributing communicative factors, that we come into contact with, in everyday life, dispenses what is true and what is not. Choosing, seeing, sensing or not discerning what we confront, and how, will determine our growth rate or shrink rate, is Jesus our all in all or do other things still have hold on our heart. When a person is not true to who they are, they experience limitations due to misperceived reality. Such as the law becoming our tutor to lead us to Christ; now in Christ we've a direct relationship and are no longer the tutor. People follow religious beliefs a miss always learning but never coming to the knowledge of the truth. Religious beliefs or other darkened thoughts of the world, Evolution, vain philosophies, etc..., which offer no rest, we're to learn of Christ Him only. Then when a person confronts their limitations in a loving environment, are around people who patiently show through their character there's a better way, they come out of denial and regain control of their true identity (space). Part of strengthening identity comes from strengthening a center which as a review, is comprised of emotional and logical reasoning capabilities. A damaged center as in the case of a child whose parents never reflected an orderly stable character, (such as a Christ-likeness), cannot express its emotions rationally. Instead, it just acts out and rides the fury of whatever that emotion may be, resulting in further darkness entering the space (love without truth). Logical reasoning on the other hand, without emotions, can leave a person distant and cold and out of touch with their needs and the needs of others (truth without love), and when it interacts (abusiveness) more darkness is laid into the space as well. Strength to a center comes from bringing the emotion and logical reasoning together in a constructive way. When confrontation arises it is necessary to express the emotions through logical reasoning.

Example: Anger (to keep the problem from growing out of proportion). A man finds his girlfriend has been unfaithful and rather than confront, he carries the darkness of his emotions within until his anger rules him and he shouts at everything and everybody losing himself and everything else he holds dear. "Let not the sun go down on your wrath." If the same person confronts his girlfriend and says, "I'm angry and disappointed with you; you've really hurt me," then by speaking the truth, he loves himself enough to protect his space and more light enters his space and he grows from the situation. Now with more light (truth, wisdom, knowledge), he can better decide how to handle the situation. The key factor is the spoken word and the action he took for the final creative power which is produced. The battle is for which force will control the tongue: light (life) or darkness (death). Here is an equation which best illustrates the components at work.

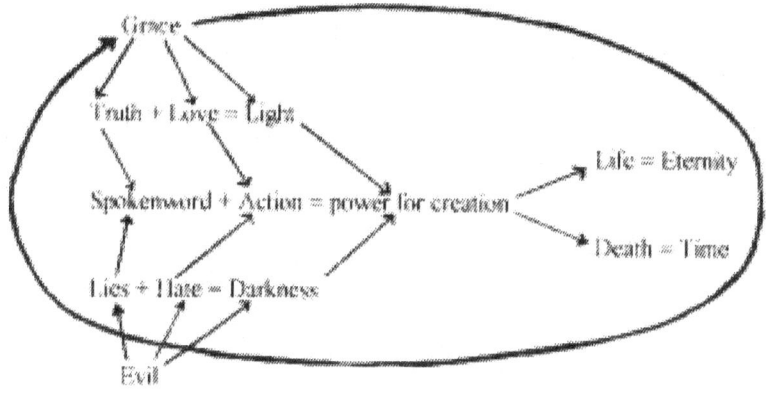

Psalm 17:2,3,4 Let my sentence come forth from thy presence, ...I am purposed that my mouth shall not transgress. Concerning the actions of men, by the words of thy lips I have kept me from the paths of the destroyer. The mouth is a gate for beings (light vessels, dark vessels) to enter and exit throughout the power of creation system. The way we conduct ourselves according to our character is always sending off a message. Most of us are unaware of this interaction with self-conduct and others, one on one, within a group or even how we take in mass media, such as TV, radio, movies, magazines, or even read a book. If conduct does not line up with God's word it's going to lead to destruction. Mat. 25:29 For everyone that hath shall be given, and he shall have abundance: but from him that hath not shall be taken away even then which he hath. Our true vision should come from peace and contentment in God's power to change us to recognize His voice when problems arise and obey no matter what the outcome may look like. God honors His word we need to look here to trust Him as He carries it out. When we hear God's voice, how hard of listening we become at times. Darkened distractions become a way of life till God finally has our attention. We live in God's voice, His spoken words and actions gives us pure clarified existence with Himself,

"man does not live by bread alone but by every word which proceeds out of the mouth of God," unlike darkness which distorts. We connect with God's reality through Jesus Christ, living word, we become a part of His body. I'm living inside God's voice and it sound mindedly sounds good inside my mind. I let His love control me, His promises are yea and amen for we are still living in bible times. When a truth system is in proper working order, Eternal truth which has balance with a love-filled space, and a logical control of expressing emotions center rather than acting out, then light is produced which breathes life into darkened spaces. This establishes structure, order and stability for other controlled centers we interact with. However, if truth or love are not found together, then the reality shifts a lie becomes the center of a limited space which is sectioned off, or hate-filled space, then darkness is produced and sometimes as appearance of light, (angle of darkness disguised as an angel of light). The language is that of lack of control for it cannot see the light in what it says but only speaks to gain attention to itself and create a counterfeited self-centered light. A person whose incomplete goes out of their way to get attention to feel accepted, instead the creature worships itself rather than the creator. Whatever controls the center controls the tongue which bring into being creatures for life or for death. Whenever Jesus spoke light went forth through power for creation, people's circumstances and lives were changed, and the forces of darkness was pushed back. When Jesus spoke to the fig tree it withered and died. He further stated if you have faith and you say unto this mountain be thou removed and cast into the sea it will be so. In Mat. 12:36, 37 we find, "but I say unto you, that every idol word that men shall speak, they shall give account there of in the day of judgement. For by thy words thou shall be justified, and by thou words thou shall be condemned." The thought may come to mind who then can be saved, remember with God all things are possible, amen. I call on Him daily.

3

Space Survival In Unreality

Reality is Truth + Love = Light which is eternity. Eternity can only be obtained by grace. Grace gives and fills with light as it meets the needs of people who are takers, (dark spaces), which fill till they overflow so that they become givers of light and life also, self-seekers become changed in this way. It's a gift and it is always present and waiting, outside the time dimension to join us together through reality to make us one with itself, apart of the body of Christ. Reality has peace and no unrest. Unreality has no peace and only unrest (Love + Truth + Lies + Hate = Darkness). In darkness the more we struggle the more powerful the darkness gets. When I am true to who I am my space breaks unreality (Darkness) and through Jesus I join Eternity. An example of this is prayer, and as it's been my experience it joins us to eternity. Even when we pray for something to please the flesh God works in us to desire His thoughts of light more, then we lose interest in what darkness has to offer.

If person A. wants to know person B.'s reality, when they ask something of them, sharing each others reality, person A. must stay contained in their space. When person A. sees person B.'s space is not equal to his own growth rate conflict arises. Prayer must take place to bridge the gap to be respectful of each others' growth rate. A space that is full of light is in continual conflict on all sides and without guidance form Eternity, it will fall prey to be filled with darkness. If conflict is not handled properly a space's light will start to dim. When the space realizes the light has moved, the space speaks the truth of his error (repents) and then is rejoined to enternal life. Being true to who we are in Christ, more than our old behavior, causes us to grow closer through truth constant to reality which teaches us how to love ourselves the way God intended, precious and free from the bondage of sin.

Walking with Eternity is not burdensome, for love strengthens and gives life by enlarging our space, Jesus carries our load. He says "Cast all your cares upon me." The devil wants us to focus on our cares that we'll have no time for God. With Truth + Love = Light there is order, every part of us is in our proper place, we work properly, no darkness disrupting our space (friction and stress) to break things down and cause malfunctions in our systems, to bring death. When we think clearly and love correctly we're able to avoid destruction by following God's guidance and end up in safety. Whereas in the past we would have passed on unable to recognize harmful or abusive people and get punished. The wages of sin is death but the gift of God is Eternal Life.

Stars that don't move hold their position and as part of a solar system it holds its planets in an orderly orbit. Even molecular structures such as atoms have a nucleus center with electrons in orderly orbits. When the atom is smashed a violent chain reaction takes place. The outcome is Atomic bomb deconstruction. Without order addressing the truth of another person's reality, how love should be applied, there would be damage to both spaces. When someone is not feeling safe they'll always turn to the most balanced point for stability, thus restoring peace and order as rational reality reference. However; unless Jesus is the continual reference point, structure will have no stability and remain a lie, no matter how correct or assembled over numbers of years credible, it may seem. When the blind lead the blind the two fall into a ditch. Damage happens one line of darkness at a time. When we over-extend ourselves beyond the limits of reality, such as having priority needs to be met, which will cause the flesh to say me first. Like being hungry, tired, falling behind schedule for added pressure, etc. It is here our space will be worn thin and open to penetration from darkness. Prayer is essential for rejoining ourselves to eternity and having our peace and order restored. "Peace be still and know that I am God", puts God at the head, this reality should happen to us. As we perceive the peacefulness of eternity our actions connect with love, this produces the light of life which enables us to work stress free. However, when unreality says we have to make things happen, our peace gets disturbed, that is not true to who we are. The response to such conflict for me is that may be true for you, but, I've not grown there yet, I can't just go somewhere without growing there for to do so is to become off balance again and live a lie. Right now I've got to do what's right for me, keep my peace for when it's easily disrupted uneven growth will occur. Trying to make reality happen is second-hand truth and there is no revelation in it as we lose sight of God. Love and truth have gone out of line, leaving darkness where there was once light. When truth is experienced first hand, when experiencing confrontation, our response towards truth constant causes us to be sensitive to God's love which produces light. When we answer this light our relationship energizes us as we draw closer to God, and grow one line of truth to an understanding as to how God has just met our need, where we couldn't and He clothes and protect us from further darkness. It is at these times of reflection that we stand at the edge of His reality and discover whether or not we live in God's country, to experience the embrace, His love. If you want something right away you must wait till you grow there and not just go there. When we try to exceed our limits without waiting for growth, such as disrespecting others when we tell them something they don't want to hear, they'll tune us out when love is not present; we enter unreality and leave our outer perimeter, hedge of protection, and reach beyond our growth point. This puts us out of order and opens us to attack from darkness. Darkness always makes pretenses as to something it's not. Loud, voicetrous, important or powerful when it's really just as a worm which hides from the light beneath the rock. Light pierces darkness. Darkness with its intense hatred toward love, it tries to suppress all of love's advances. For when enough light burns away the lies, this will expose the hate so love can be applied. Then darkness loses its ground and light starts to build. Although darkness tries to sever, disconnect, light from God to break the bond, so it once again can bond the space to its own darkness. Darkness has no order because it has no light to see what it's doing. A space will only survive in unreality if it's connected to the Light = Love + Truth. In this light a space can see its order and know how it operates drawing from an Eternal reality apart from time base perceptual unreality. If a space loses

15

its order it no longer belongs to God unless it cries out for help. For the son of God has come to save (bring into the light) that which is lost (in darkness). Calling upon the name of Jesus, re-entering the door, always brings us back to His world. God is so good, His grace is amazing.

4

God Will Only Be In Control If You Let Him

God's Eternal reality is true and in order, time base unreality is separate from reality and not in order and therefore a lie, counterfeit, contrary to be able to produce life. A man raised in unreality has no or very little patience, is a liar, a thief and a murderer when he reaches his full degenerate ungrowth state. Jacob is a man who filled this description and God loved him. His brother Esau had a pretense of being good and God hated him. God can work with somebody who can be true to who they are. To be ME is to hate and lie which is to be true to who I am in an off balance world which is out of order. To ask God to change me to be me in Him, in everything I do, is to be true to Him by honoring Him above my ways, which are limited to a time based dimension V's God's Eternal world. Little children know how to turn to their father and ask for help. Understand we're little children in this time based world and we need to ask to be taught how to survive. There's no life to be gained from the things of time that don't agree with God's word. You can't just go somewhere without knowing to where you are going to, or you'll miss eternity to be duped by lie + hate = darkness (the devil), and be his slave in a limited space time dimension. When we touch the reality of God we are able to speak His language of life which keeps back the forces of darkness. What fellowship does light have with darkness, a kingdom divided against itself cannot stand. We must recognize that within our space we have an enemy at every turn that wants to fashion our clay vessels, as Adam was made from the dust of the earth, into children of darkness rather than children of light. The devil lies to us to instill fear in us towards the eternal reality of our living God. When truth gets distorted there are misperceptions of God that scare people away, when actually in God's reality He holds life and in the devil's reality death. Jesus knew we would make mistakes and bring shame upon ourselves while being sanctified, but we're still holy and righteous because of His blood which is shed for us on the cross. By grace we're able to see we've taken our eyes from the Master again, gone astray like lost sheep, and be restored to the truth of the new us in Christ 'being found' again to graze in the safety of God's pasture of life. Once we come to trust that God, Love + Truth = Light, is more valuable than who we are as children of Darkness = Lies + Hate, the devil, then we are set free. Jesus said, "Come unto me all ye who are heavy with burden and I will give you rest." When we let God have control of our lives, the life that God gives lifts our load that the devil wants us to carry.

Acknowledge Him in all thy ways. Lean not on your own understanding and He will direct your path. We are set free from Lies + Hate = Darkness by acknowledging God's ways above our own. Not relying on an understanding which puts our thoughts above God's. We turn our control over to God's and He directs our paths and a maximum of what life has to offer is ours, grace and a free gift. God's mark of proof, the death, burial, and resurrection of Jesus Christ our Lord.

5

Transformation

"Forgive them father for they know not what they do." Eternity looked out over time and saw man's darkened understanding and knew by planting His seed of light, all men would come unto himself to escape the darkness and death and enter into the light and life Christ has to offer.

Transformation comes through faith, many who took and take God at His word and believe, which sets aside the first to establish the second such as when Abraham left his dwelling place first to follow God not knowing what was next. It caused Him to exceed His limits one truth at a time. As Light = Truth + Love, is perceived as reality, and when darkness becomes diminished by Jesus till non-existent, a part of transformation takes place. This is where confrontation is accepted as God's property and trust in our fleshly selves dies. A new perception happens where light as life is born and our lives become enlarged.

If we take a look around us, seasons with the change they bring, will show life and death on the move. The moon from new to full shows a progression of changes taking place. We are always growing and changing as well. A child sees actions as incorrect, they're not obeying, nor being loving. Through transformation, children are open to rebuild, incorporate correct love into their identities and become obedient as a natural more healthy way of living. Bit by bit a child grows by listening and watching and copying everything. Oh that they see God's pardon of sin. As we have been forgiven, shown mercy, that our children in turn will show mercy to others. Are we as role models in touch with what they hear and see? We transform others as we are transformed.

It's a chain reaction, the transformation process, where death and life cause greater understanding. Our naked rotting bodies are starting to be clothed with light. Old things pass away; all things become new. People see the rottenness of their bodies when exposed for something wrong, sinful, they're caught in the act. Light shines on the perpetrators, opens their understanding, leaving them vulnerable, exposed. For these people see themselves for who they really are. They see rot and smell its stench. Culprits feel they'll be rejected for their crime. However, the reality is that when they see the truth of their condition and confess it, there can be change.

It is the nature of Lies + Hate = Darkness to try to cover up and recapitulate the situation, to move towards more darkness and keep away from light. The devil prejudices our decisions by limiting our options. He tells us to keep hiding, running or lying and we won't get caught. Behind every spoken word there's a structure which backs it up. When our words don't go beyond the end of our space, rejection is experienced and we've exceeded our limits. If nobody wants to hear, than our own words respond by backing up into our own thoughts. Darkness tries to prevail, prayer is needed to correct the growth of pressure, a problem in our space until we reunite with eternity. Jesus, here is a man, being one with God's word is a structure which produces life in everything He says and does. This carries over to the infrastructure of transformation in situations. If you know how a person functions when they're in order, such as Jesus, then when one part is not functioning properly it's easier to find the problem. However, all of life is a problem and we look to where conflict does not exist. In our relationship with God, God produces a need, which man chose at the fall of Adams' disobedience. The need is conflict. Through conflict there's a confrontation which produces heat. In the heat of any situation we're shaped through spoken word + action = power for creation. In this reality a bridge between a world of unreality and eternal reality are joined. I live for Christ through Christ.

Transformation takes place when darkness is removed and light takes its place. ".....I will guide thee with mine eye," says God in His word. Do we follow? Where else do we go when He has the words of life.

At one point in my life I had a song and couldn't sing. I knew it was there and yet I couldn't get it out. I was afraid of the darkness around me. I did not know where my song would go to or how it would be received. I needed the safety of God's structure and did not know it, but this voice came out instead, "I want attention, I want the spotlight, it feels good to be accepted by others. I want everyone to know how great I am. It's an elevating experience which makes me feel in control of everything and everybody. Let people come to me. I want to show off and get attention." I wanted to make up for what's lacking in my life; the child that was never ever nurtured or cared for or had experienced being a healthy child.

Past wounds need to be healed by applying healthy structure a little at a time. Trust and respect must be established with that structure in order to replace the unfulfilled needs of the past. First we must recognized that our past is out of sync with our present. When we realize we act out and do not take action for correction we go into denial. It takes God's eye, to see light, and move us in the right direction, or we'll go blind due to a lack of focus, deception takes place, darkness prevails and we are deemed socially inappropriate (sinners). Then face, confront, our past and accept it with love and truth together, in order to integrate through Jesus and transform through His Light = Love + Truth so healing and growth will occur. Light will interact enlarging us spiritually and generate energy through spoken word + action = power for creation. Now as apart of the light, separated from darkness, I can see who I'm returning my affections, my heart's song to, the light of Eternal reality.

Light!
Intense Light!
So Piercing,
So penetrating,
So Beautiful....
Light, becoming life
It breathes strength into my soul,
I'm on the other side looking back at me,
At last I'm free.
In the land of the living
Everything breaths
In the Dark

Yet continually guided by the light,
Little by little I grow
God Kept His promise, I can see,
On the last day I'll arise.

Clear sight as a healthy perceptual balance is obtainable providing it can cut through an out-of-order time-based unreality and build vision in the eternal reality of order. When love and truth embrace with a kiss, perfection, light is produced which burns away the darkness of time and opens the Jesus door leaving order in darkness' place. The things of God in the spirit now start to replace the affections for the things of the world in the flesh. Order has been experienced and chosen over disorder. John 2:15 Love not the world neither the things that are in the world. If any man loves the world the love of the Father is not in Him.

Jesus leads people out of their present structure, our familiar Godless idolatry darkened thoughts pattern system of doing things our own way. He brings us into His way of life to work His life-giving character in us as we walk with Him. It takes time to recognize God's spirit is telling us not to go back to our old lifestyles, but in the process we experience pain to let us know we're not on the right path. God is patient with us while we learn and He gets our attention by asking, "Who do men say that I am?" As if to say where else are you going to get your directions? To be swayed from this point of view is to accept the flesh in time as natural and not the spirit, the things of God from the eternal's reign. 1 John 3:9, 10 who soever is born of God does not commit sin; for his seed remaineth in him: as he cannot sin, because he is born of God. In this the children of God are manifest, and the children of the devil: who soever doeth not righteousness is not of God, neither he that loveth not his brother. I love the truth and the truth loves, as a part of the truth which I love, I must love too or then I'll be a liar and no longer apart of the truth which I love. Therefore God's word being truth becomes my actions carried out and my words, as I love truth we become one. God takes on my sin and cleanses me with His own blood, then being joined to His body as a part of His body in His spirit I carry out His will.   John 13:20 I tell you the truth whoever accepts anyone I send accepts me; and whoever accepts me accepts the one who sent me. As we seek the light of love and truth, growth in every area of our lives, (spaces), starts to transform us towards Eternal perceptual balance. When we have eternal balance our reasoning and emotional centers are at rest in the center of our space. After a successful transformation takes place a structural transfer causes permanent change, as when cement is set, it becomes stone when the undisturbed conditions are met. Two structures that exist since childhood are good and evil simplified. Within a good balanced structure when the basic elements are in line, linked together, God's spirit flows properly (maximum light) as when Jesus shown as the sun at the mount of transfiguration. Peter, James, and John were brought into eternity as it touched time, Moses and Elias talked with Jesus before their eyes. Then Peter opened up his mouth with time-based reasoning, "Let's build tabernacles for them," and God pointed them back to Christ. Eternity proceeded in and with Christ as he stepped off the mountain and encountered a demonic boy with his father kneeling at His feet saying, "Lord have mercy on my son." "All things are possible for those who believe," was Jesus's reply. Then the father cried out with tears in his eyes, "I believe..."   (your reality) "...help thou my unbelief." I want to enter your reality, show me how. Mark 9:25 when Jesus saw that the people came running together, He rebuked the foul spirit saying unto him, "thou dumb and deaf spirit, I charge thee, come out of him, and enter no more into him. Again Jesus's action and spoken words can be found yielding power for creation to go forth. Eternal light comes in pushing out the darkness which once again gives eternal life restoring order. The spirit cried out shaking the boy all over and then came out of him. The boy didn't move so people thought he was dead. Mark 9:27 but Jesus, (eternity), took him by the hand, and lifted him up; and he arose. As we look upon Jesus the part of us that believes is the real us which holds life. As we yield, God possesses us. God establishes a tabernacle with us and dwells in us. Psalm 43:3 send forth your light and your truth, let them guide me, let them bring me to your holy

23

mountain, to the place where you dwell. We are invited to set up camp, in an on-going relationship with God during our habitations here on earth as long as we call out to Him in time of need, thanksgiving and praise continually. I'm learning from moment to moment there are needs that have to be met and learning how to bring them together is where we meet reality. Jesus came to serve, as we call He does just that without expecting anything in return. (I don't have to but I want to now that I'm able to love). Just to believe in Him, the light of the world, and let Him put all your darkness under His feet and be saved is the only requirement, which brings God joy.

In an evil structure, God's spirit is there but not invited in. People who are in darkness experience fear of the unknown without God's guiding light. Darkness tries to put out all light, keep a space blind and completely possess it or it tempts it into exceeding the limitations of its growth rate, to break its contact with God. The bottom line, it wants control, it wants your life. Darkness tries to get us to obtain something we're not ready for, then our center shifts in our space towards its outer limits. If the space does not repent admitting its mistake and return to order, which is to ask for help from God's reality, then Lies + Hate = Darkness is open to come in because the space through its hypocrisy is hurting itself. If further denial occurs the space takes on a false identity. A structural breakdown within the spaces center, as when we put our thoughts above God's, and causes a false center to shift into position. With a false center in possession the light center gets imprisoned or choked out within its own space. When this happens, we live to please the senses of the flesh, reasons and emotions get mixed from love and truth to Lies + Hate + Love = Darkness. The demand for reason kicks in, we as reason try to find out what has happened now in the dark. Falling over its edge reason sees it has become unstable and a correction to fix its disrupted structure must take place. If reason tries to call on its own resources it will land on another plain of unreality and further darken its understanding. However, if reason realizes that its structure is out of order and cries out to Jesus, who is the light for help, then reason can see the wound in its structure and ask God to change the tear from evil to good with its light. Order is then restored from disruption to control and rightness. When walking with God, if you go where God is not, then God is not going to follow you. Things are hidden in plain sight and you must stand still to see them. Standing still creates confrontation with darkness causing friction where our habitual behavior is tested, the way molecules expand when heated so do we. Growth is at the door which generates further heat we start to swelter, a call to return darkness' last attempt to eleviate any discomfort, which generates Light = Love + Truth which brings opportunities for change and for further growth as we can see ourselves for who we really are. Grace is then experienced, as the price of peace brings us peace and the sanity His order brings.

6

Space Extension

Space extension takes place as we develop from truth to truth overflowing into Christ's character as natural. Christ's character dips into the chore fibers of our being. As He touched me I knew what was lacking in my giving to others. I could only give what I was capable of giving and no more. I could not extend myself to others because I was limited, nobody taught me how to give. I'm angry that my caretakers never "gave" love to me. Only as I forgive them, the floodgates of my love slowly are opened, that I may live again to give again in the trust and care of the Lord. As Jesus melts my icy heart and reveals my life was never woven into a pattern for appropriate behavior. I was left stranded, to fend for myself, I'd very rarely connect with others and confusion became a standard for a way of life. I did not know how to spend my time or what time well spent meant. I now know it's important when talking with a person to know who you're talking with. Am I meeting their needs? Am I communicating my feelings when I confront or encounter with another person? Am I being true to who I am or do I go out of my way to accommodate other people in order to get my wants or needs met? Extending ourselves to other people should come from a solid core of peace, a sense that everything we know is in order and confident that we're real people, Christ centered. Then when people come calling for service we can acknowledge them and minister to their needs, being a servant of all, reaping eternal life's reward. How people respond to us is an indicator whether or not space extension is taking place in a healthy way. Are we truly chief among men? Are people comfortable around us or we them? What is learned from examples as we copy or are copied from will be sewn into the heritage of our lives. The fabric of truth and love should bear witness with others as an overflow from our space one area of growth at a time, extending outwardly, welcoming others. A genuine relationship with God will cause growth in every area of our lives. Full first, then to overflowing; meeting people where they're at in a non-intrusive healthy way.

Energy is never used up. It's either transferred or stored. For every action there's an equal and opposite reaction. We all pull and contract off of each other however, when Jesus is the center of control of a life, whoever accepts that person is being drawn towards Jesus. Jesus said, "As I have loved you, now love one another." People reflect to each other their actions and spoken words, this is power for creation, which generates conflict resolutions. This weaves different fibers of identity into each of our beings causing catalysts for change. As the timing of the conditions for change are met light permeates other spaces, very few are aware of what's happening, as they are drawn to the space with the light. The end result is a spaces' fabric, filled with threads of light which are extended towards where darkness once ruled.

When we see the beauty of God and are filled with a growing knowledge and understanding of His grace, we're introduced to a relationship with God Himself, which takes place where there's a putting off the works of darkness. Such as fear, pride, etc... for we walk in the light as He is in the light and there's no more room for darkness in truth constant light. The more life is extended from a space and interacts with others the more life we will cultivate. The rewards become greater and greater and the glory is always returned to God, for even more dividends. Ultimately God's Eternal Reality will extend itself over Time Based Unreality, and what it has to offer, bringing Eternal Life wherever He flows.

7

How Much Are We Worth In the Kingdom of Light? (God's Kingdom)

We need someone else's opinion because in looking at ourselves we cannot estimate our worth. God suffered the cross to mark us with His blood and open Eternal Light to us, that's how much we're worth. In God's kingdom of light the high king Jesus reflects his image and glory to his subjects, those who believe Christ for salvation are the lower kings. With every new experience a thread of truth or darkness, based on conflict resolution, is sewn into the kingdom of a king. Our bodies, our members, our fabric is a kingdom. When a king behaves less than his true worth, as a slave, infiltration of his heart and mind takes place. Darkness then has its way with him. After this no one will want to hear this king. They will no longer recognize his true value. We value ourselves according to riches we've in ourselves. Only the light of Christ inside us shines brightest. Light must uphold truth and love, to keep its value, which pertain to us while we find our way out of darkness. This is the path. Our truth must recognize Jesus, to be able to grow and increase in value. No deviation from truth constant (the Holy Bible), should be made, or deception will tarnish the truth creating a dark lie. Such as to go off on a tangent, a crusade, to see where the winds would take us, while all the while experiencing our king's worth at peace is where we belong. When we live a life in darkness, there is an oppression from the truth of the love of His light (Jesus Christ). We know He's there in all His glory, yet we feel like we don't belong. His order has not yet found its way into our hearts. We're used to darkness and its devilish lies. As in the bible story when a son who squandered all his father's early gifts of an inheritance. Because of his mistakes, due to poor judgement, he felt worthless and could never return home. Then the thought, (a thread of light), my father's servants are eating better than the pig slops I'm eating now. A long way off on his way home the father received

news of his son's coming and organized a great feast. Then the
father went to meet him and fell on his son's neck and kissed
him. "You've returned!" The son was looking to return as a
hired hand 'if at all' for his king's worth had been devaluated in
his own eyes, but not the Father's. "Into thine hand I commit my
spirit: thou has redeemed me, oh Lord God of truth." As I look
upon you only then am I real and possess life. "Whom have I in
heaven but thee." God touches the heart and illuminates His
presence. "God is the strength of my heart and my portion
forever." "Be of good courage, and he shall strengthen your
heart, all ye that hope in the Lord." God's light is the only value
that lasts. "I have put my trust in the Lord God that I may
declare all thy works," and feel thy wealth.

One ray of light rules over all darkness yet darkness lies and
convinces us to hate Christ's light. When we're alone and under
attack, we draw closer to God; however, the devil brings an
oppression trying to convince us our relationship with God does
not exist. Once we get free of the devil's grasp, we've to escape
his kingdom of darkness with continual prayer.   While
journeying onward in His light, the light of Jesus, we must be on
the watch that darkness does not come upon us suddenly and
ambush our growth.

There is safety in the multitude of council. When two or
more come together in His name, agreeing in truth, His power
reveals to us our shortcomings. This increases our value, as
darkness is pushed out and we invite change to bring more light
and shine our worth reflecting His glory. It's often hard to
maintain an attitude of truth, staying in the light, with familiar
voices of darkness calling us away from appreciating to our full
worth.

Jesus said, "It's more blessed to give than to receive." We
must remember that Christ's light itself increases our true value.
Sewing fibers into us to show in us His worth of His kingdom
that he shares which extends us outwardly towards others.

When we lose our way (or balance), we call for help. Light
pierces darkness, causing us to stand again as we feel our true
value, king of our kingdom, return. We are hammered out into
greater value as we venture onward at all costs, leaving darkness,

to obtain more light which we see along the way as we continue to grow spiritually. Our desire to live according to our Christ-given worth, even though we're living in a worthless world, except for that which Jesus luminates in it. To try our own or any other way is to denounce the light that is within us, and cause our kingdom selves damage. We state our worth when our past history is changed. I'm no longer an adulterer or have a sexual addiction, I have eternal life and a sound mind. When darkness leaves and we see our present is new, this proves increased value.

Darkness tries to devaluate us by causing us to forget our past growth. Prayer keeps past and present worths linked together. With every new experience we gain and add towards our worth, providing the confrontation adds life, with the King of King's light. We realize our salvation gives us worth when death is replaced with life, darkness with light. We see a difference and know a royal proclamation has been made. We are kings. We have ministering spirits to reinforce our new identity to shine in the kingdom of light. Darkness flees leaving its slaves behind, to be recovered and glory in the value of the freedom in the light.

Darkness threatens we'll lose control of our relationship with Jesus, our value, if we don't follow after the light. Don't be driven; God will lead us by His grace with His peace. There's a self deception to want to ask for approval from darkness to leave, but you won't get it. Darkness will try to blot out all light and sever your true value.

Now that we've our royal value we may want to show it off. Unfortunately, you can't force someone to know your worth. Be patient, ask God to guide you, and wait for the appointed time. You also have to trust the light of God's word to be able to change other people and let His Spirit do its work. In the meantime, your majesty, enjoy your position in the kingdom of His body of light and pray every day to remain joined. In prayer we're to believe the things that we say shall come to pass, without doubt in our hearts we shall have whatever we say. Jesus states, "What things whatever you desire when ye pray believe you receive them and ye shall have them, and when you stand praying forgive."

Remember the next time the devil asks, "Who do you think you now are in this madness of your false perception?" You simply answer, "I am King (<u>your name</u>), child of Jesus Christ, cohier to the throne of thee living God. Rich in mercies, Ruler with Eternal light over all the unreality's of darkness having received the gift of Life Eternally forever. I now have true perception and unfailing worth, as I drink from the fountain of living waters, wearing the crown of life upon my head."

We have Eternal worth, we live forever, our value never ends, and everything done with Eternal vision is done with honor. God is in control. In the world everything is temporary. Manipulation of its elements, sorcery, witchcraft are without honor. Material possessions such as cars, houses and even fame will come to an end when time runs out and everything enmeshed within it. God's word stands forever true, don't be deceived into thinking otherwise. Know where you stand and shine forever, too. Where timebase unreality ends eternity begins.

8

Feelings

My views are distorted from warped emotions which consume my thoughts. A tangle of jumbled feelings displaced in an out of order box.

I believe there are correct choices I can make, only I'm not in touch with what they are, to give me a better quality of living. I'm limited in my understanding and can only see through the parts of me which have been luminated by my best choices, God's word. Poking my head into God's domain I'm not used to His order. I wait and I watch for the correct way to go, understanding perfect peace with contentment brings eternal vision. As God's word states, "Thy mind is kept in perfect peace whose eyes are stayed on Thee."

Applying God's truth with love is essential for growth. How am I loving and honest with myself and others? How do I confront the truth of others in situations which arise without giving my relationship to Christ, my life, away? These questions are connected to the way we think, our thoughts, and the way we emote our emotions. There's a need to bring them together to make the best choices for ourselves due to damage which occured in the dark recesses of time base unreality apart from God's domain.

Feelings are thoughts which perceive emotions spontaneously. Each thought ought to be connected to an emotional base which brings stability and adds structure to our lives. Each emotion to a thought built upon honor having sight of eternal values. Feelings are made of a fabric which is cross stitched by our emotions and our thoughts. When conflict arises stress depresses the fabric of feelings, and our thoughts and our emotions process according to the aprior knowledge which have been collectively processed before. This building block process, when healthy, will establish a woven pattern with all our thoughts connected to our emotions.

In an environment where stress is always present there is a continual depressing of the fabric in which processing is never allowed to be completed. A warp can cause emotional unbalance which can disrupt the spontaneous connection between thoughts and emotions. This damage inflames, like a bruise, our emotions are separated or detached from our thoughts and it effects our thinking and how we relate to others, God included. Stress upon stress over a period of time depresses us to the point of being overwhelmed. We become fearful, due to the overload, and shut down by further detachment from our emotions to protect ourselves. Furthermore, when our emotions are not allowed time to process, we carry a warped perception to other situations as well, furthering our damage which distorts our point of view. Our inflamed emotions blinds us as to the full spectrum of our other emotions which causes us to set unhealthy goals which are deemed by us as healthy. In a system stressed to fatigue it becomes difficult to process anything, for emotional inflammation desensitizes the connection to our thoughts.

In the end result of this condition our thoughts which dominate with inflamed emotions give one message and our other emotions another as to which direction to take. Once thoughts start making decisions without healthy emotions the damage only becomes worse. On top of this when a circumstance arises that's too fast to process, sudden death of a loved one or a bad accident, thought patterns can become severed and the fabric torn. Stability of the present structure becomes lost and needs to be rebuilt in a way that will promote healthy growth.

There are both healthy needs knowing how to receive love which build on connected thoughts and emotions and unhealthy needs, unable to receive love, which cause us to make decisions to fill the void of the empty torn structures. Whatever our choices, we build into who we are and how we will grow. A warped perception causes us to go farther and farther off in emotional balance, until the load of misperception goes so off, the person topples because of the weight, (has a nervous breakdown).

People who are downed due to misperception will not be able to get up again until focus has shifted to something or someone, God included, as substantial which will lift, a little at a time, that person to a healthier growth perspective. Things with substance reinforce or add to our identities and help us to grow. Substance, our heritage, happens as eternity touches time, this reality starts the growth process. This suggests change, not just a reinforcement of the current structure, can take place. We are to feel our emotions before God's word, talk them out patiently loving ourselves in truth; this opens Jesus to us.

People who blame God, by pushing away what is eternal, cover their mistakes so they can feel more acceptable to themselves. This blinds their reality to limit truth the way they want to see it. This in turn takes away love which leaves them void and without eternal light, the life line. Pain takes eternal realities place when we don't realize how we blame God. By denying who He really is we set destructive behavior patterns in our heritage. We trust our ways more than God's word and heritage. This cuts off a relationship with the life giving and living God.

In time the brain is an instrument, a preceptor, which integrates the past which gives way to the present. Particles of truth pass through our minds and influence our reasoning. All thoughts are spiritual and either expand our understanding or contract it as lived by producing more life or death. My mind cannot comprehend Eternal Reality fully as the more I grow I realize how much I don't know. This leaves me vulnerable and open to attack in the areas of my life I don't comprehend eternal realities giving light. Condensed life comes from a structure enmeshed with eternity which order gives us insight towards our present burdensome disorder. Making straight chaotic thoughts is one step towards healing our damaged feelings.

First we have to see our problems, then we have to see a sample of how we function, properly, then build by asking God to change us from our shortcomings towards the healthy model. Seeing problems can be difficult as people do not know they're not feeling their feelings. When stability of the present structure is lost a safe non-hostile environment will promote growth, when people are away, as in all relationships, fibers are interwoven, and enmeshed, depending on the duration of time. It is harder to grow when connected to foundationally unhealthy people who keep tearing us down reinforcing hostile behaviors to ourselves and others. Even the wrong TV shows or unhealthy radio songs can be stifling. For healing we should spend time around others who have an interest in being connected and are willing to share how their feelings come together. (Jesus) is an honest role model to guide us back to health. Learning about Jesus produces in us the things we know we need. When we're in the midst of a difficulty or struggling with something in our personality, we need to keep looking where we belong, into the mirror of God till we find ourselves in His likeness, His character, and are changed from our old nature, its lifetime of dysfunction, there are freedoms by God's grace here to become new. Rest, exercise and diet will help to reduce stress also. Furthermore, healing also occurs when shortcomings like tears in our fabric go from being filled in with Time Based Temporal Darkness which keeps thoughts and emotions from connecting and lives in our spaces that has not yet healed. To Eternal Light Reality from Jesus which promotes insight toward healing by drawing thoughts and emotions closer together through sight from His light. We also need a vent to let off steam and reduce stress. I find prayer important in this matter. Inside expressions not spoken out can make us physically sick, suppression pushes feelings further apart. When we wait upon God continually and have His love, His peace, His presence, we know when something disrupts us. Seeing and knowing when we're disturbed causes our emotions to connect to our thoughts and we speak out truth and love which come together to build more eternal light immediately. This protects our emotions sparing us pains which may exceed their healthy limits for growth. Once we learn our feelings are censors that warn us of the unpleasurable circumstances of life, then we won't go to an area of discomfort once again, repeat the same mistakes, where as in the past we'd pass on and get punished. Now we know that there are consequences that keep us in check, restore order.

Damaged feelings leave us prey to any unhealthy situation that may arise. For we fail to sense what leads to emotional pain and are unaware that they need to be trained to function properly. Feelings do not operate, as we know, when they become stressed out, when exposed to unusual amounts of extreme pain. Much like hidden pressure building beneath the surface of the earth, its outcome always leads to destruction.

Once emotions become inflamed, cold and distant from thoughts they only come back to the healing warmth of God's loving touch, through other people, or Himself directly. A person has to get honest about where they're at, stay there, without detaching emotions from intellect, remember how far they've come (track record), to remind themselves growth is real. It is encouraging to know God Himself has bought us thus far because He loves us and desires a deeper relationship with us. Here are some indicators as to whether or not God's spirit is flowing, to direct us:

1. If I'm uncomfortable I'll not move till I'm sure I'm feeling all my emotions honestly for any given situation. Do I feel my words when I say them? Am I in touch with them as I let them out to others or in prayer with God? Being in touch with my capability to love others and myself also is an indicator of being whole.

2. I'll take inventory to see if my thoughts are connected to emotions. "Can I express them or are they missing?" Be at peace and absorb each situation although long pauses in speech can suggest detachment from reality. Separation due to inflamed emotions cause misperceptions. This keeps us limited to a time based reality bringing chaos to where order should be.

3. Am I over extending myself and going beyond my realities limitations when I'm not ready to move?

Learning how to make correct choices with the full range spectrum of all our thoughts and emotions connected is an every day exercise. It prepares us for what Time Based Reality, and everything connected to it, will bring our way as we grow eternally against its current.

God keeps us complete, "Stop trying so hard you've been going through the motions of My presence lately without Me being there." "Be still and let Me love you. I want to spend every day with you if you'll let Me, remember Me, I am the Prince of peace, your direction for life. I'll not go with you where My peace is not present. Now come let me hold you and you hold Me, it's gonna be alright." John 17:26... the love with which you loved Me may be in them, and I in them. We have a relationship with a living God. As I hug Jesus who is in me He hugs me back through me as He is in me by His word become flesh. I can also see Him looking back at me with His gaze in my eyes in the mirror in my reality reassuring me of my growth as a new creation in Jesus Christ in this way I'm a complete person. Gal. 5:16 We're to walk in the Spirit that we do not fulfill the lusts of the flesh. The Spirit bearing fruits of love, joy, peace, long suffering, gentleness, goodness, faith, meekness, temperance. To go astray of intimacy with this character is to go outside the will of God which first brought us in, and invite harm which can happen if we don't recognize we've stepped away from these fruits, our source of completion in life. Mark 14:38 Watch ye and pray, lest ye enter into temptation. The Spirit truly is ready, but the flesh is weak. II Tim 3:16,17 All scripture is given by inspiration of God, and is profitable for doctrine, for reproof, for correction, for instruction in righteousness, that the man of God may be complete, thoroughly equipped for every good work.

9

The Last Dot
#12. *We were never created to be alone.*

When God said let us create man in our image, God's image is plural. We're created to be plural as well. Adam in his fall, when he partook of the fruit of knowledge of good and evil, allowed evil to enter himself for the first time. He lost the purity of righteousness and felt naked. The righteousness of God, the Holy Spirit, had departed and he was left alone. Now Adam feared God and tried to hide, for he knew he was no longer a reflection of God's image, "His Word" and became troubled at God's presence.

When sin enters our thoughts it creates holes in our mind, like cavities in our teeth. Places where God's eternal word reality does not exist but should. Sin eats away at our life, lies to us to keep us away from God's word, a door to enter the Eternal, and erodes the truth of a righteous character away to close the door to the Eternal. This leaves us hollow, empty on the inside, starving to death for life. "A little leaven, leavens the whole lump." With righteous character, we're full, solid with order, dense with life and contain it. This gives no place for the devil to come and steal our lives. Psalm 40:13 surely the righteous shall give thanks unto thy name: the upright shall dwell in thy presence.

People are always saying, "Come be a part of my world. See what I've created and accept me, approve of my kingdom." While all the while they're being cheated. For their little kingdom is a room for rent. It continually needs fixing, paint and patching. We try to busy ourselves with people, places and things to hide our nakedness (fears about sin). The same way Adam did not want to lose anything, he tried to cover himself up with fig leaves, a quick patch. While God wants to give us many mansions, with gold walls and a climate controlled roof and make us a part of his Royal family, we inherit all he has to share with us.

The big picture is to focus on God's world not our own niche. Trying to get everybody else's approval of how great we are, to try to make our rental world bigger. John the Baptist said "...that I may decrease that Christ may increase." People want to hold, "have," thinking it's theirs. Things only occupy an empty space as does anything that does not belong to God, that when we die we're filled with unbelief and belong to the father of liars instead of the Father of Truth. We must give thanks to God in all we do giving the glory and ownership of all to Him. Jesus, who leads the way through His grace, invites us to restore our righteousness if we follow Him in Holiness. Jesus opens the door to the eternal and holds it open. This allows us to encounter and be clothed with the Holy Spirit which restores us to being plural.

As I see, know this, to live is Christ. His character in us yields substance and holds eternal life. Just as brushing my teeth keeps decay from making cavities, reading God's word protects our souls from spiritual decay. A vessel to honor holds life. Just as a vessel to dishonor holds no life; it is out of order and full of holes. I cannot trust the thoughts of men for there's no life in them. Lord keep me I pray, I watch all the spiritual flows around me and sometimes I feel alone as I'm tempted to enter in. Then I remember it's death to touch the unclean thing, realizing my eyes have strayed from love, the Prince of Life, I grab hold and return with Thanksgiving and my joy returns. Lord go before me in all I do, let me be mindful we belong to you.

My mind has become a map, I must be careful what I draw on it with my thoughts or I'll be lead away from Jesus the Eternal. I see now that the Eternal is forever and time passes never to be regained. If we are linked to time, live in its reality and what it has to offer, then we become temporary and pass at its end. What is Eternal, the reality of God's word, which lasts forever, holds the immortal and everything connected to it. For eternity displaces time, it creates a pocket where there is no life and becomes absolute life everlasting, Eternal life. My body will pass away but my spirit will live forever with this promise: The inheritance of an eternal incorruptible body to reign with Christ forever.

"Peace be still for I the Lord your God have spoken. I heal all hearts that seek me and bind all wounds."

> Love sweet Love,
> Joy sweet Joy,
> I am made whole, I'm plural now,
> Clothed with the Holiness of God,
> But once I was broken.

10

Prayers, Poems and Visions Through Growth

1.   Lord, I'm in a lonely place
the desires of my heart unfulfilled
but then I consider your ways
and I'm found content
as your spirit flows over my soul.

In the midst of the storm
I feel your peace
and it is only you who are carrying me.
I have no strength to go on
I'd laid down to die
never to arise again
had your spirit not lifted me.

I love my breath as I breath I know
you gave all of them to me.
Now I am pumped up with the knowledge
of your grace.

God has not forsaken me
in my time of struggle
I'm tossed back and forth
up and down
my peace is disrupted
help seems so very far away.
I remember my strength from above
and I'm held by your comfort
as I leave my life the way I know it
I see my future
and I know what life lays ahead.
an open door to eternity
a pin tip of faith through the clouds
lights the way to bring me all the way in.

2.   I saw the light
even now as I am in the light
It first shown out of darkness.
It lit the way for me to go
that I may follow
from the darkness till the light
diamond bright beautiful
A star rested upon me
and my brother
we both shared how darkness left
Now as I am still
There is your peace.

Oh! My Diamond light
I want to embrace
to know you are there again
but then I see
you've always been there
It's me who had not been still
Oh how now do I enjoy you
as I embrace
where truth and love are joined
to be filled
only when
I cry out for more.

Oh my lord
I know you're with me
My King forever I would like to serve thee.
Keep me joined
Change me so I'll not be moved
I want to stay with you
but I am weak
never too weak to call upon your name.

3.   I feel like I'm dying
Being stuffed down in a bottle.

I want to run ahead and shout
I'm alive, I'm alive!
It's not over I'm alive.
Growing in a different direction
is what this is all about.
There is no life without death first
Dying can be claustrophobic
So settle down and die
so you can grow again.
raised from the dead
Allow yourself to be fitted in.
It'll feel good to belong to what's alive.
To see through eyes
full of life
smiling bright
now my fears are gone
dying has become a sweet song.
Unfortunately, I've to wait
Can't pick the time
Fortunately, I can be glad
For I know what's over there
shines brighter
than the best
what's over here.

4.   I know there's more to life
than what meets the eye
But I want to see the whole picture
as I patiently wait,
what are the battle plans
when and what is it
that's going to cross my path.

Continue to be patient my child
and do not concern yourself
with matters that you cannot see
or the enemy will divert you
from the plan.

You may know
the more dense with love and truth you get
the more the enemy is displaced.
My light shines through you
in a darkened world.
be still, let me be your peace
as you move about
you'll be in my kingdom.
Watch for my signs
and I will continue to guide you.
when patient you'll see,
understanding what you see will bring knowledge
The knowledge will reveal who else is in my kingdom
or on the way there through right actions
which will exhibit self-control continually
keep pressing on and you'll find great change
take place, where you'll find a healthy love towards
others and you will all slowly be joined.
all standing still and encapsulated.

5.   Distractions are a way of life
when joined together
they drown out who we are,
jumping from particle to particle
in a cloud of dust
we miss the beams of light
that shine on by.
I'm a sunbeam rider
so much room to move about
and be so free
there ain't no particles on me,
joined to the light of creation
I can see the particle people,
how miserable they are
locked away in their darkness.
Show 'em some sun and they'll
up and run, or their whole world
will fall apart, sounds like a scary thought

what makes particles so inviting anyway?
Just specks of light
reflections,
imitators of what is real
but is really not
imitation life,
it makes me mad
especially when
a particle tries
to land on me
but it just burns off.
I'm a part of the sun.
Looking back I say it's sad, but true
I was once
a particle person too.
Discovered the light I did
and what's real
is better than
the imitation
if you'd trust
and just let go
and be joined to the sun.

6. I fell
which in falling
I can see
a planed pattern structure
where my thoughts cross
cross my emotional cords.
I land as I watch
what's on my mind
my eye looks back at me
and I laugh for all the joy.
Bright, bouncy light
and yet not all of me
not in touch with
all of me yet.
My emotions are not all there,

some have grown distant and cold
They need to connect to be warmed.
But how?
The maker of the machine
can fix them!
Just need to know Him to ask.
Here He is now,
come ask Him how.
Wow! I see all the order
of His kind gentle face
there's no need to fear
my cords draw closer as
I feel His love embrace
I'm damaged from the fall
I say, can't quite pick up myself
and run proper as I should.
Then the maker answered me.
You my child are gonna take time.
You'll be fixed but you've got
to trust me it'll bring you peace
and when you're completely
standing still...
I'll know you are working
and sense you with thrills.
I'm lifting back up now
not far of a climb
as long as I'm held
by the Maker and trust
that he is the Craftsman
and creator of man.

7.   Oh Lord
I do not like
the place that I am in.
Have you tried
being alone with me?
Lord I need you
ever before me

at all times.
To punch a hole
in this reality of mine.
I see things in my future
that are unpleasant to me.
Can you really see
what is mine alone
To reveal to thee?
Look to me,
and your reality will change.
My views are distorted
from warped emotions
which consume my thoughts.
A tangle of jumbled feelings
displaced in an out-of-order box.
Lord, I need you to move on me,
to lift my lid and show me
how to make things right.
My child it's already begun,
For now you see what's going on,
be still now and receive my love
enjoy my presence above your own
Let me hold you in my trust
and you will be made whole
Oh Lord I'm still and...
Put down your pen and I will
tell you when to take it up again.
Have you not enjoyed my presence
more than life itself?
Yes, Lord I have. The heights,
the depths and the width of it
and now my box has been made whole
just as you've said.
Now, remember, I am the vine
I alone give life.
As long as you are connected to me
and draw from me
you will be my branch.

Take your mind from me
and you'll by no means
have life, you'll wither and die.

8.   The worm turns and eats away
our precious thoughts of love and peace.
When it is finished,
what once was sound and true
will cave away with hollow residue.
The worm of death which comes in
from the pit beneath the recesses of time.
How did this worm come in?
Through untrue words, thoughts and deeds
which we heard or saw as we live and breathe.
There's no way for us to reach in and get it out
Take away the lies and get them out! No! Falseness
rules.
Where am I to find a way?
To reverse this process of rot and decay
which blinds my mind with stings of death
and keeps me restless with no rest
I want this worm, I want it out!
Then read God's word the Bible, without any doubts.

9.   Paralyzed with hypnotized eyes
I could not move or see
Beyond the reality of this fear.
I could not sense as my life
slowly, painlessly, started to leave,
squeeze by squeeze, and tighter still
I did not know to run or where I'd go
so stay I did and rest on the coils of death,
still unaware of the snare.
Then he caught my eye and broke with light
my paralyzed sight, the frightened stare.
And filled me with the strength of His life
which broke the coils of death
of years, so many, unaware.

His heel does crush the serpent's head
and sets all captives free.
For it's only the ones set free that talk
the rest, poor souls, get swallowed whole.

10.   I'm not ready for life,
still in badly needed repair
forced to go on
no relief, falling apart moves
downed low energy operation,
rest so far away.
Where's my help?
Oh, how we've danced
by the light of the flame.
I looked at you, you looked at me.
The love of a dance
by the light of a flame.
I entered in and stretched out my hands.
I bid you to come
and to burn in the flame.
you backed away
somewhere into the night.
then you were gone,
no longer my song.
Now I do stand
in the light of His flame
ever to burn
Yet I'm not consumed.
Still in my mind
as you've faded to night.
Though I do burn
makes it hard to see the light.
Being rebuilt
takes oh so much time.
Though I do stand
How I'm running my mind.
Now I'm learning to close
to the things that I see

and watch as the flame
has its way
within me.
I am engulfed
I watch as I burn
my senses renewed
as I rest in the flame.
I see the fire burn in my eyes
my space is enlarged
as I now know thy name.

11.   I've lost my way
I've lost my sight
What could this misperception be?
How and why is this happening?
Darkness now cuts me off
It blocks my way.
I look back
I trace my steps
wrong turn, wrong turn right
then I wait and watch.
Be sure to stop or you'll miss it too,
something beautiful, something new.
The bark peeled, fell off in chunks
away, away, the tree has fallen
and beneath the pile of rot, decay
a little green sprig of a bud
it lives, it grows, it shines
Now here comes the golden sun
to light anew the way to grow.
It is by grace we start afresh
your word have I hid in my heart
I stand in awe as I watch and know the way to go again.

12.   Tears flowed
as I cried
At its best it was mean
at its worse it was death.

The anger burned inside
Out through my eyes.
Yet I was powerless
within myself there
was nothing I could do.
so I slayed the lamb
to appease my pain.
As I cried out the blood flowed, aloud I cried out,
everywhere was splotches of red
as the blood dripped it collected
a puddle royal red upon the floor
From out of the puddle a lion arose
sent forth into battle where I could not go.
Now I was calm as I put forth my trust,
I rested my head where I thought I would bust.
The victory's mine for I gave Him my load
As he carries me through I know I will grow.

13.   When I was young
dazed and confused
made messed up beds
bad for the head.
Too many rocks in my water
to see clearly to think.
Couldn't be still
wouldn't be still
I knew all the answers
no one knew better than me.
Rebellious no love kid
who defied gravity
pushing onward and upward
Forward to make my mark
gonna take the town by storm.
But nobody noticed
and I was destroyed.
Look here I am, the further I got
the bigger I was
an image of projection,

who took away my silver screen?
Now I am still and I doth see His face
as I shine like a diamond reflecting His grace.

14.   I'm less than myself
Torn into two
strength all gone
To want to go on.
Deflated from life
yet forced to move
I've got to be still
get in touch with what's left.
Part of me hallow
no balance in step.
my center is here
but the rest is not.
I leaned too heavy on
the promise of man
a support that would not last.
A step and a shift
now I'm on the right path
onward and upward
he never leaves
as he guides in His light
I'm being filled with eternal life.
to build on and with
an everlasting last.

15.   Emotional rest
feeling secure
like a scab
falling from a wound
you're making me whole.
I'll always remember the cut
that hurt so bad.
All of me gushing out
for days and days on end
comforters consoling

tender touches
here and there.
But my master's hand
such sweet embrace
holding me, holding me still,
so the wound will close.
you know my soul
and what it will stand.
Now as scars
upon my heart
which I hold dear
to see
where your love
has left its mark
Now apart of my life
It gives me life
no longer an open sore
I'm starting to fill
with your presence
once again
as sorrowful grieving
gives way to calm
I'm now in anticipation
of certain joy.
When your wind
fills my sails
I'll be ready
to journey further
But right now
I'm content
to wait here
with you.

16.   There's a well that I draw from
whenever I thirst.
It's a good feeling
to know that it's there.

better feeling, just when I need it.
The more I come to understand
this well
the more I want to drink.
Water: well up inside of me
so much I want to share,
but others don't understand
the thirst.
They'd rather I be me,
at best, I can't say they're wrong
If I'd just slow down
and feed them salt
perhaps then they'd want to drink.
Being me I've got to see
when I am drinking
I am me, content and satisfied.
Otherwise I've got to wait,
still no one comes
Where's my patients?
the well is there
surely they'll be others
who'll want a drink
like me.
So I stay at my well
and I drink
the only drink
that has ever given life.
I've learned
to take my eyes
off of others, to enjoy
and talk
while drinking
splash, water, splash
coming up
from out of me.
The well's not mine
Now I'm the well's
the way it was meant to be.

but I get lonely when I wait too long
so I step away from well watered well
"This way to the drink I say."

17. Your wind blows
and fire burns
within the bosom
of my soul
Though all forsake me,
as to leave me for dead
I will stand
for you are there.
Though troubles wash over me
more numerous than the stars
in the sky, while I am drowning,
I know you are there.
Wind blow wind
fire burn hotter
when sickness comes
and my strength fails me
as long as there's a hot coal
I'll burn eternal flame
as I call upon you
my breath returns.
The light of my life
returns, and the beauty
of my eyes shine forth
your loving kindness
Taste of truth sweetness
adds substance to my
body
which causes me to
grow
closer to eternity
your peace restores my
soul
Now I can contently see

the way to my new
home.

18.   Cut to the core of my innermost being
I bleed internally.
I can't stop my feelings as I go with the flow
My tears wash over my soul, again and again.
In search of an answer to my pain
as my life continually moves ever forward
The past is but a moment left so far behind
but as it breeches the present, my future lit by past,
becomes
bigger than life which wells my tears as floods come
gushing out.
Then the tide recedes my present is back
The screen in my mind plays an image of my scene
I watch it way back there, all those years
now they're gone.
Shuffled into place as I grow from state to state
I have moved on.
Incorporated feelings I know that they are there
in touch to feel again
ready for another special place.
apart of God's plan.

19.   Upside down slide
Inside out walk
spun around
to walk straight
in which direction
no direction to take.
I've tried them all
They lead back here.
To a blackness thick
a decayed goo, blink
Wait a minute
I think I see

a hole which leads me
to darkness side in
light side out.
Too scared to move
For I don't know this place.
So used to
closed tight nitch
now it's gone
I've got to trust
for life to go on
I must live
with a walk
that's in sight of each step.
This new world is unknown to
me
full of light and room to move.
Yet the nitch and the dark
hold my hand, fear
I won't let go!
yet I must to grow.
Suddenly, I sense a warmth
that says it's OK to be alive,
to come away,
leave it all behind.
But is it real?
Is it true
to say good-bye
and start anew?
I spread my wings
and sense they're real
the colors, freedom in the air
I am made new
my load is lighter
sweet flower nectar
my life is brighter.

20.   Pain!
       Killing me!
       I'm torn open!
       Inside broken man.
       Can't get the pieces together
       to go on.
       My song is gone
       My heart is cold
       Suddenly I feel very old.
       A flower past its time
       Pedals limp, fragrance gone
       dried to the bone
       They crack and chip
       fall apart
       I can't get up
       to move on.
       Where is my God?
       I need you now
       I need your light.
       I need your life.
       I need your love.
       Have mercy on me
       that I may be spared
       this living Hell
       of feeling feelings
       to despair.
       yet they're mine
       and I need to know
       they're there.
       How else could you make
       me whole?
       How else could I grow?
       I see now
       It is your plan
       I know you're here
       I understand
       To give it all
       and then to trust

that you're the master
and I'm just apart
of Your plan.

21.   When I am still
        I am complete
        Ahead of myself. Mania
        disrupts the perfect order,
        displaced bubbles
        tossed crazed madness
        In out of order order
        all is made right.
        Cheap second-hand copies
        walking falsehood wise.
        I'll never give in
        I'll not detach
        I'll move with extra care for that.
        What am I doing way over there?
        I've opened my mouth and let
        any old words come out
        I've made a mistake
        why that just isn't me
        Now I'm character captive
        in a false identity.
        Please let me explain
        I'm not who I seem
        why I've been put to death!
        It means disrupted dreams.
        Back tracked traced truths
        I do believe an apology
        is in order.
        For in order honor order.
        It all lines up
        all figures out.
        Now I walk while
        standing still
        and trust track steps

still peaceful still
and trust track steps
I am not mad but carried
complete, for eternity
views
all of me
with every move I make
yet not I as seen
but the invisible visible
which grows and lights
my way
to walk in peace and
stay
complete. My moments
are becoming slowly
joined,
the more I know, the
more
I grow as deeper love
doth find my soul.

22.   To see wrong and not correct it
is to do wrong.
To correct incorrectly is to do wrong
when correcting a wrong.
Peace displaced is wrong
correcting with peace is correct.
Have to maintain true peace even if it means
disrupting the peace I already have.
This is not an easy task.
I know the truth about this place.
About decay and rot and death.
The forest of the ghostly trees
Darkness looms with hate and lies
a sandy desert of stubble growth
where hot winds blow to cause distress.
People filled with lies they walk as not to see.
They grasp at air and call it wealth.

There's nothing for me here, I stop and stare.
I see your light a door from here, another world
where colors swirl and people bubble up and sing.
Alive with life, all the grass is a true green and trees are trees
Eternity has opened up for me and when I die
that's where I'll be.

23.   Let it ever be known
that I do have needs.
But where to bring them to
has always plagued me.
Fear of rejection has kept them inside
and beneath the surface of me I hide.
It's hard to trust,
yet I've got to, to survive.
To learn to bring my needs to God.
Instead of carry them up high.
Upon my shoulders till I carried the world.
Now when I have needs
I get them met.
I speak my piece, soft not loud
I watch, I wait where peace doth rest
upon my soul.
No longer inside hide but in front of truth
I let them out.
For I know I'm loved no matter what I say or do.
Not perfect yet as revealed by light
Alive and well in all our sight.

24.   I rejoice at your touch
I thrill at the rest
in the palm of your hand.
A time of joy and peace
to celebrate in praise
with thanksgiving in my heart.
And it's true you are really you

the beginning towards an end which
meets my means each and every day.
Too grand to be contained
and yet content from day to day.
As I grow I search for more
and as I find I am enlarged.
Mmmm. Feed me now to be complete
I sense your presence coming down
you make me whole with your great love
and craft with truth the way to go
From darkness dark unto your light
which shines divine, supreme I sing
I'm filled so much I overflow
Two hungry souls which start to grow
which in turn rejoice and thrill
to your marvelous light from beyond
and above, it's your higher ground.

25.　　Eye sky eye
beyond eye sky
black void empty
only darkness inside
Then came light
distant sparkle
in my eye
light side in
I see clearly now
Dark side out
Just a dark dot spot
It reminds me
of where I've been.
I'm alive and I see it
I know where I'm from.
The door of light
It shown so bright
Now that I'm here I want to...
No, no, no I'm out of order
with the light, but how can I stay.

Can't change myself
to fit in the right way.
My clothes are as rags
I need help, I plead!
I beg!
what is the promise
that I have to know?
To stay where the light
doth cause me to see
to belong in the land
of the living
where I'm full to
overflowing
and connected, I belong
I feel my tears when I
cry
I know they're mine.
The joy and excitement
all at the same time.
What must I do
as the black spot doth
grow.
I see you have tried
I see you've cried
You know you can't
stay.
Now look this way.
Peace be to you; rest
upon me
Be still and know
that I'm God, come to
trust
and know me by name
Then you too will
belong.

26.   In the silence there is movement
        the space between the lines
        the ones that are missed
        never to be read
        and yet there's life there.
        I tell you I have seen
        and yet so few believe.
        Unseen space between lines
        there's a battle raging there.
        Voices whisper to our thoughts.
        If you can't see the voices
        and know where they are from
        Then dazed crazed madness
        leads your life to a destruction.
        The darkness says let's keep him numb,
        while all the while truth is still.
        The lines they move you till you're through
        If you try to stop and stare
        the voice will speak where you don't seek
        There's no between don't go that way
        Come stay this way, let's laugh, let's play
        But I've been there between the lines.
        How else would I know that life is mine?

27.   Slow build grow
        a sure foundation
        is a place to be
        especially when tested
        and you come to know
        when it all burns away
        in the heat of all your days
        that what is left
        is going to last.
        and what is here
        is becoming you
        As you stand faithful
        to what is true
        All the love

inside of you.
It warms the darkness
of all the coals
till they melt down
to diamond bright
This life that I speak of
cannot be compared
with anything this side
of this dimensional world
yet I enjoy it I do
as I partake of all that's You.
Eternal life
which warms my soul
and precious blood
which glues my bonds
and holds my bones
as marrow transplanted
asunder from down
under
replaces life with death
It's hard for words
to express my gratitude
of knowing you
To feel complete
I'm home at last
It's by your name
my mighty savior
It is Christ Jesus
My mouth does savor.
I taste your spirit
it is so sweet
upon my heart
I am well fed
and all of your works.
I watch and grow,
as You it is I know.

28.   I have a vision of time frozen
　　　　Order restored Eternal flame comes alive.
　　　　Time standing still unravels you see
　　　　and its thread is reformed through the door
　　　　a shuttles beam which undoes disruption
　　　　a name above all names which puts off corruption
　　　　where wrong is put eternally right
　　　　and truth is no longer a fright in the night
　　　　but flies high as it soars by the truth by day
　　　　It is light which is good and dark that is blind
　　　　Be kind to the tree which has birthed thee
　　　　Be cut from the death
　　　　and joined to the life.

29.   I've seen life
　　　　though some try to deny it.
　　　　I have, and am living in the real world.
　　　　I entered the door through the written word.
　　　　It, the word, stood up and embraced me.
　　　　I entered this land one line at a time
　　　　then followed its light
　　　　excellent and pure...
　　　　Darkness light mind dims,
　　　　where there is no life,
　　　　tried to get me to doubt its reality.
　　　　It is not there, how can it be?
　　　　Why everyone would question your sanity.
　　　　You'll be alone, you'll have no friends
　　　　What have I now?
　　　　I'm going after eternity!
　　　　The beads of truth I taste which get on line
　　　　to form a thread they are sewn in
　　　　This brand new life which pushes darkness
　　　　to destruction's end,
　　　　I am brand new as I fight and stay
　　　　Life everlasting eyes perceiving clear
　　　　the way I go I acknowledge God
　　　　my breath is His, for honor has all His saints.

30.   As I cry out I'll stay forever true
       I press forward to the mark of the high calling
       From light which makes up love and truth
       to glory to glory which expands
       connecting me I am restored
       Yes I've seen life at the vine
       grafted in forevermore, to be content
       where my substance is full and not to be ignored.

For This Prayer Read Out Loud

31.   With a sincere faith and a clear conscience
       Lord I ask for your Glory to come down.
       I invite your spirit to come into my midst.
       Lord keep me ever mindful that it is your
       righteousness and not my own.
       Keep me from stumbling or wavering to and fro or up
       and down,
       Cause me to truly see the full price that was paid
       It was your blood shed on the cross for me
       You bought my freedom and broke all the chains.
       Now give me your resurrection power to keep me
       Free me from all the death of my flesh
       so I may receive the fullness of your life.
       Keep the song of your presence in my heart
       and my fire and hunger for you, alone
       burning more fervently for you each day.
       Keep me watchful, alert and ever mindful of your
       narrow way and keep me on your path that I
       may be found ever pleasing in your sight.
       Cause me to stand still and know that you are
       God and master over my life.
       Jesus govern me that you may love me with a fullness of
       your measure.
       You're so patient, merciful, kind and generous
       in all that you've blessed me with.
       I thank you my living God

for watching over me.

32.   Your judgement is so far above our understanding.
Continue to bring gladness to our souls
in an ever-increasingly hostile world.
Always keep us teachable
that we may walk in your true humility
and get to know you and your ways
which are higher than our ways,
better and sharper as our time with you
marches on.
We love you and, we praise you, and we exhalt
you Jesus, the best we know how for
evermore, it is the reality of your words,
which bring life and to no other place I will go.
Amen.

33.   Lord Jesus, your great light
shows me my nakedness and a blindness
as to a way to even clothe myself.
All I am learning to say is to be merciful
and clothe me.
Teach me that I may no longer feel naked in your
presence. Lord Jesus teach my mind to be still.
I can still see doubt, fear, pride, impatience, distractions
an affection for my ways in the heart.
Lord take out this darkness so a fuller
measure of your light may come in
and I ask you to keep it in.
We speak to God with every thought we think.
Our words when we speak them He hears us.
If we admit that we're talking to Him
we get His righteousness, protection, and life.
If we don't admit it, and talk in the blindness of our
ways, we lie and get blinder, more darkness, less
protection and then finally death.
Speak as unto the Lord.
Let's light the way

by following Christ.

34.   Oh Dear Lord Jesus
        come and lift my heart.
        Before I stumble down into the pit.
        My heart took the burden
        instead of you.
        Now I've lost my way.
        Come and see me through.
        I can see your light saying
        Come to me
        All is forgiven
        I'll see you through
        Don't be shy
        open up your heart unto me.
        I feel your love
        Thank you dear Lord for providing
        Jesus your cry for me
        and your tears are living water
        which keeps me from getting burnt.
        I say to Satan, "You're a liar."
        My love holds me and His name
        is Jesus.
        The chains have been broken
        and your glorious presence once again
        floods my soul.

35.   The shallows of the heart
        the doubt in the flesh
        can interrupt the fullness of our
        spiritual life.
        A spirit of forgetfulness
        shouts at me, screams throughout the day
        Now let me handle it
        I've got everything under control
        My thoughts from the grave.
        Then the spirit of destruction comes up against us
        and tries to get us to look away from

our life-giving Jesus, no way I'm here to stay!

36.   All my heart I give to you
        All my heart, you'll see me through
        Oh my heart, How I love you
        Give me more of you
        so I may love thee more.

        Keep me in a fullness of your presence
        Guide my steps and still my tongue
        So I may rest in your love
        all the days of my life.

        Man was not made to lead but follow.
        Children learn through imitation.
        If parents never get beyond childhood then
        their children will not grow much further than their
        parents.
        However, when God is truly the parent, the
        things of this world can't possibly interest man.
        For he's too busy growing on with God to
        look back. God will only be our parent if we let
        Him. When we hold onto anything this world teaches
        through the eyes of a mere man, (the devil's pawn)
        then we close ourselves off to the fullness and
        newness of life that God wants to teach His children
        each day.

37.   There is growth when all earthly, worldly
        distractions are removed from the path of God.
        All affections, attractions, and any other self-seeking
        pleasures
        or indulgences must be removed by asking God through
        the blood of Jesus Christ as He (God) reveals them to us.
        For to make a self effort to try to put off sin is to deny
        God's sovern power over us.
        Oh Lord you are God, Oh God you are the Lord
        Yes God is there but is he your sovern Master?

38. Oh my song, my love, my very life.
    I cried unto thee
    and you heard me
    you've delivered me
    I shall praise you always.
    Even in the face of my adversaries
    did I praise you.
    The roaring lion became
    a gentle kitten.
    But even cats scratch
    so I continued to look unto you
    and all became quiet.
    Not no one can stand in the light of your presence
    My King of glory
    all darkness leaves
    those who stand and are not moved from the light of
    Your presence become as shadow people.
    When the enemy tried to follow
    I turned and looked to you all the more
    and you sustained me in the midst of the heat.
    Even though the very flame of hell itself
    beat about my brow I looked neither
    to the left nor to the right
    and when doubt tried to breach me
    and pride I confessed my fainting
    straightway to the Lord
    and he honored the honesty of
    my cry all the more and lifted
    me to the right hand of His throne
    where I kissed my Lord
    with the love of my heartful yearning.
    Then He bore the weight of my load
    and slew my oppressors till they came no more.

39. Lord I'm like a dead man without your presence.
    Where is my love?
    Without you I only know death and blackness.

Where is my King of glory?
What have I done to offend my Mighty Warrior?
The heat is turned up and now I realize I'm not burned
It was only the flesh trying to make me feel uneasy.
I see you at work still patiently building me.
Still teaching me to stand still
and sing praises of victory and praise
to my only possession.
I depend on you oh my Lord God.
Deliver me from my circumstances.
Quicken me, to trust fully.
My Lord has heard my cry and moved mightily.
Thank you Lord for sending your
angels to bring peace and order to
my life once again.

40.   You were innocent and you died for them.
       You were innocent and you died for me.
       You said, "Forgive them Father, for they know not what
       they do."
       Now I say I forgive them, too.

41.   At one time I had loved certain things.
       At one time they gave me joy.
       But now the things that I had loved
       were sins in the eyes of God.
       It is a narrow road unto salvation.
       But I know my tears
       shall one day turn to joy.
       To lay down your life is hard to do
       but easy in the sight of God.
       My reins are being tried
       by thee Almighty God.
       My heart does tear on every snare
       as His ways are often very hard.
       But the more I surrender
       the easier becomes my walk.
       joy starts to flood my soul.

Now where once I walked I run.
The arms of my blessed loving savior
are getting ever closer unto me.
For I know one day, that the trumpet will sound
and be heard through all eternity.
Oh to feel His still and peaceful presence
every time I come across an object, my past
reminding me of dreadful days.
Now I rejoice at last.
When I stand before my Blessed Savior
and He sees that I do have no past,
He will say, "Well done thou faithful servant.
Enter in, to my land where everything lives."
Though my flesh still tries to fight me down
and my life still tries to hold its ways,
I am mindful of the King who is my Master.
Then I am weak in the greatness of His name.
He knows all the secret places of the heart
that only He can bring to remembrance
for the complete freedom of all of His ways.
Jesus the light of the world.

42.   Man has made many filters and devices of his own.
Ways to see the sun, but with the naked eye it is not
possible without harm. Other people not only take the
sun for granted, but during a very dark storm no
thoughts of it ever return, for they get too caught up in
the thought of the storm. But after a storm an occasional
puddle of water might reflect the sun's rays and again
bring it to remembrance. During a sun shower it's not
unusual to feel the drops of water in warmth of sunlight,
and be quickly reminded of the sun's rays due to an
unusual phenomenon of circumstance. When it gets
very cold, one quickly can become mindful of the sun.
Unless there are clouds which, over an extended period
of time can make one forget about the sun again. A
snow storm is much like a rain storm. Only after a snow
storm, the snow reflects the sun so brightly it can

actually, in an instant, blind all our thoughts with a painful glare. A sunburn can be painful, but the sun never shines on the inside of us. However, God does. Just as there are many climates all over the world, some fixed and others alternating in its relation with the sun, so we too can be like the Bermuda Triangle in our relationship with God. Just as people can assume they are safe if they find the best place in the world to live, and seemingly have all the answers to their immediate needs, a sudden storm can so easily beset us and destroy everything we quickly lose sight of all. (Oh Jesus your awesome Holiness frightens me in my mind, and causes my soul to shiver, but then I remember you in my heart as my friend as well as Lord Creator Master, I am comforted). If we stand with God, then whether it be a hurricane of poor health or the economic collapse of the world we are truly safe from any storm. How foolish are those who have had one Bermuda Triangle experience with God and are completely lost in an unexplainable storm center of lovely living conditions. Build themselves a tower of Babel, of their own devices and ways, for God to only come and knock it down again. There's no sure safety in man's seemingly pleasant ways. For just as the Bermuda Triangle seems like the most pleasant way to man, God in His mercy will veer us away in a triangle with a hard bump on each turn of the angle, to try and wake us to the path we are on. If we were to venture into the center of our seemingly pleasant way, and forget God altogether, the Devil would have us to chomp on in eternal damnation. When the sun shines its brightest, we can see the waves of the heat in the distance, which would not ordinarily be seen. When the glory of God truly outshines all of men's thoughts and ways outside of His way, then and only then can men be saved.

43.   My Love is my strength
        My Life is my strength

My Lord is my strength
He watches over me
When Jesus is my sight.
My God is my strength
He watches over me continually I'm His
He doth answer me.

44.   Whenever my life's not easy
I ask my Savior, "why?"
He answers me with His sweetness of love
and gives me newness of life.
Gives me newness of life.
Gives me newness of life.
Gives me newness of life.
He answers me with His sweetest love
as he doth restore my soul, He keeps me whole
and gives me newness of life.

45.   Oh, Lord in my heart I have dealt falsely with you. I've
seen what you want only I've not trusted you to produce
it in me. At times where I thought I'd be pleasing in
your sight, I justified my own means. I'm humbled at
your coming as it will come to pass. There's nothing in
me that ever be found exceptable, as I am corruptible in
your sight. Be merciful unto me and change me. All I
want is to be a true sheep and nothing more. All glory
and all honor to you.

46.   Vessels to honor, vessels to dishonor They are being
filled to yield life or death set in position as the battle
rages in war perhaps honor will be maintained or
restored. We clash and scrape; grind away dull or
sharpen to a point which pokes a hole with the friction of
the heat as it pierces the darkness and enters into light.
This is where the vessels are filled with the glory of the
soul or back away into darkest night. To embrace the
light when darkness comes as it pushes against our life
and fight as it threatens sanity a fresh supply every day

feeds us and keeps us bright by grace as we take hold by prayer.

47.   I'm understanding hunger
       I'm understanding pain
       I understand that there's a place
       that goes by another name.
       Where joys abound instead of fears
       and patience satisfies my needs
       where past realities clashed
       part of the battles of days of old
       I see by vision of the light
       cutting the cord of dark by night
       I'm now where I want to be
       Beholding beauty eternally
       The more I see the more I like
       Now that darkness is ruled by light.
       and what is real is what is right
       Better than yesterday's sting
       Now I've life to take the place
       of death by enchanted night.

48.   I'm sure
       I'm confident
       in that which I know
       to be true.
       That life comes from above.
       The kind that's made of love.
       In the stillness of the night
       there's a fright we've to fight.
       It says all alone
       you'll always be.
       But do not fear
       or believe these lies
       for comfort's here
       when God is near.
       He always sets everything right
       and causes evil

to pass as the night
to places where
they look again
to enter in where love is cold
and is not real.
These are places that distract
and keep us full
but not of life yes I'm sure.

49.   The wind blows and the leaves start to fall
the decked out trees with many splendors
have lost their substance, yet their purpose remains
Now unclothed, like skeletons they stand.
They stand through many dark sky nights.
when the moon doth give no light.
Through bow-breaking snows and ice,
through storms and floods they faint not.
They hold fast; they stay true to what God
has created them to do.
Rays of golden sun exhibit budding leaves and flowers
a tree's reward.
And when they produce sweet fruit
the world is better still
For as Christians turn back the tide of evil
Marching full of eyes on Christ
The battle is fought standing still with peace
A life's reward is full
Shade in a parched dry land, will people come?
What will they find on you?

50.   I can see them pressing against
the many fibers of the veil
It is dark where they are moving
each one tries to break through
some press their faces as they cameo glisten
others scratch and claw, punch and kick
but the texture is just not ripped.
I experienced the pressure and thought that this was all.

So I settled in the dark, yet still not and yet apart.
The struggle to belong became so burdensome you see
I caved in and went away,
still blind, yet I thought I could see.
Too hard, too tough a walk for me
It'll never do, there's only one who paid the pricc for me
I know He's there, the pressure told me so.
Then a consequence of conscience
collectively told me I was wrong.
Crumpled to on my knees, face
I surrendered at the veil
helpless thoughts mind become clear
my precious gift from faith sincere,
A light that I can truly see to guide my steps
as I enter in beyond the veil
with eternal steps where hope is life; where real is right
Perfected love in perfect truth. Jesus is His name.
I know Him at last.

51.   All the day long I am Love for you
I watch and wait
for you to come, my children,
into everlasting arms.
I speak to you
through seeds of thought
as you answer
they start to grow.
First the stem,
and then the leaf
The roots take hold
pushing through the soil
moving about its out and stout
alive with branches
flowers as colorful smiles
all at once come bursting out
compassion and love
Joy and peace
patience with kindness

and oh so much more.
The fruits are all there to be picked.
It only took faith,
a little seed now complete
My children grow and wax strong.

52.   You vile serpent!
You false identity self!
I'll not let you talk, to possess my soul again.
The thoughts that are not my own
I know who you are.
As darkest death
you seek a place to rest
in the hollows of our mind
to engage us in actions
which drink away our lives
to satisfy your needs
so that you'll, like a cancer, murderously grow
Unrevealed hearts fall victim
you dance and play as they naively fall prey.
A guiding pretense promise
you feast on destructions end
In out of order blindness
You lead the way to suppress
stifle all truth of Him, you'll be defeated in the end.
The Babe of eternal seed
which ripped open time
and brought glorious light
By faith I believe, and receive life from beyond
as I see through the breach
A tear of gladness fills my eyes
Satisfaction in an unsatisfying world
Reality must be real as I know I'm free,
and Jesus is the one who bought our way
and blazed the trail to eternity.
I'm alive at last. I'm alive at last.

53. Kneeling in prayer a heaviness fell upon me. I was raised up in my spirit to the sound of a loud horn. I noticed all the clocks were blocked out and could not tell the time. So I went to the window to peel back the blinds to find out why the horn was sounding. When I looked through the blinds instantly I found myself standing near the corner of 42nd Street and 8th Avenue. People were full of darkness cursing one another and possessed or consumed with the cares of everyday life. I tried to tell them about the love of God through Jesus Christ but no one would hear me.

Then I found myself standing in front of the old building where I used to live as a boy. Standing on the front porch was a hideous looking beast of a woman, my friend Dave was telling me look upon the most beautiful creature he had found. I tried to get him to take a second look but he just wouldn't listen to me. Then the beast of a woman lifted him up and passed him through and through her body and each time Dave got passed through a look of further torment would overtake him. His reply, he just kept saying, "Isn't she beautiful, isn't she beautiful."

Then I saw some people weeping in the darkness of my childhood saying, "Why didn't anyone tell us, why didn't anyone tell us!" I ran into my wife's room to tell her what I've just seen. She was reading her bible and wouldn't hear me. All at once I realized I had never left my knees, refreshed as if I'd slept for hours. I looked up at the clock only minutes had gone by.

54. I was reading in the Psalms when a heaviness fell upon me. I was raised up in my spirit and walked a few steps and fell to my knees, I was in the midst of an all-consuming fire yet I was not burned. Joy fell upon me and I arose and started to dance in the wonder of the flame. Then I saw a friend of mine, Robert, I bid him to come into the flame and dance with me but as he approached he was burned and fell away into everlasting

darkness. Then the flame spoke to my mind Jehovah Kahna. I jumped up and dove outward at the sight of the fright of my friend. But instead of dashing myself upon the ground God's spirit lowered me slowly to safety. I could hardly move so I crawled on my belly to our bedroom saw my wife reading her bible but I couldn't get her attention. Then I arose refreshed from my vision, wow I've got to read some more and a few lines down I found the verse Jehovah Kahna my God is a jealous God.

55.   I was reading my bible in the bathroom, on the toilet, when all at once I found myself traveling through time and space. I turned expecting to see the bathroom, but was stunned to see the earth disappearing into deep space like a little blue marble and getting smaller. How vulnerable I felt, but then I came to trust I was safe. I noticed I was now passing Saturn, all at once I was poised next to Jupiter. Now apart of the frame work of it all, I thought to myself I can get used to this. Then I noticed something was happening to the earth. God seemed as it was to flair His nostril and all the face of the earth was blown off into space. There was a white glow where the earth once stood and while I was taking this in a large black fish surfaced and began to swim. Then all at once a large white fish opened its mouth from underneath the dark fish and swallowed it whole closing its enormous white teeth over the dark fish. It soared up high before splashing down back into the firmiment of the earth. Then I fell from space and landed back in the bathroom.

56.   Traveling across a desert I saw a great old shoe, a boot with laces, off in the distance it stood out, covered with dirt. Then a light shown from on high and with a steady golden beam it pierced the great shoes' bronzed leathery texture. It appeared to have worn out its use with its ratty old laces and many creases, but the golden light

from on high continued to shine beneath the texture of the shoe. Then all at once the shoe began to melt away like wax and from under the leather as it peeled away it shown with pure gold as bright as the sun. Oh how God fashions from the inside out, oh how God fashions me.

57.
Front
Cover
I see an eye letting out droplets of golden light as truth. Each droplet falls through the darkness of space and time and lands to touch darkened spaces who are growing to be filled with light. People, the spaces are people, who can see the light in each other and are drawn into unity as they all grow to seek the eye which hold the order and keeps the door open unifying the light. "Thy kingdom come, thy will be done in the earth as it is in heaven." Psalm 36:9 For with thee is the fountain of life: in thy light shall we see light.
Those in the light are no longer apart of this worldly system and are passing through it seeing that light.

58.
Why is my soul disquieted within me, when nothing is too great for my God. My gaze has fallen prey to circumstances out of my control. I try to embark on a journey without God's backing and noticed my undertakings quickly overwhelmed me. I must confess I put my trust in my own abilities and now oh Lord, my God, I apologize. You've become my direction; my sight is restored. You carry my load. My soul doth rejoice as you're magnified again.

59.
My good friend Jesus how easily we become forgetful of you during the day. Even when you're right beside us throughout the day, distractions still have a place in us. I am becoming aware that you're becoming stronger in me and the things that had hold of my attention are starting to drop off in chunks of darkness. Your light in me is taking its place as is your life. Thank you Jesus for all the attention you give me. You make me feel really special, amen.

60. Oh Lord give me wisdom over situations I encounter with other people daily, that my bond with you will remain strong and my fellowship brings forth life. I enter in with praise and song with your deep abiding joy, confident You will teach me as I grow forward from this place, amen.

11

In the Flow

Mark 2:6,7,8 And some of the scribes were sitting there and reasoning in their hearts, "Why does this man speak blasphemies like this? Who can forgive sins but God alone?" But immediately, when Jesus perceived in His spirit that they reasoned thus within themselves, He said to them, "Why do you reason about these things in your hearts?... As we are joined to God's spirit we become sensitive to what is of His order and what is not in order of ourselves and others' lives. We sense the language in their spirits and then know how to proceed, how to love best the truth in any given situation. Jesus is God, He is able to know all things and as He is in us and we in Him we start to comprehend the unseen as seen. Just as we learn to speak a language we must learn to speak the language of the Holy Spirit. We must sense where our words begin and end. Just as we have fingertips with the sense of touch, our body can become sensitive to the move of the Holy Spirit. It's a battle to keep our minds clear of all thoughts and open to the word and spirit of God only. Continual prayer and meditation on the thoughts of God is a struggle which produces spiritual growth and strength, which helps us to endure all things the world may bring our way. As we dip into the river of life which flows from God's mercy our thoughts become God's thoughts which are clean, we come out new, then is victory ahead as royal proclamation goes forth we've just crossed into the kingdom of light and its rewards, out from darkness. Luke 1:78,79 through the tender mercy of our God, from which the Dayspring on high has visited us; To give light to those who sit in darkness and the shadow of death, to guide our feet into the way of peace.

What is true is solid dense with life all the way through. Lies are hollow and empty and contain no life at all, only a deception of life which caves in under pressure. Darkness feeds off of us here to drain us of our precious life. As the pressures of life, come squeeze, Lord change me to send you ever before me.

My cup runs over with joy as I see the vision as to what is to come, life everlasting, for I am well fed with God's reality.

Time is relative in eternity. What has happened in the days when Jesus walked the earth, in His flesh, is happening now in eternity. When one is connected to eternity through the living words in the bible which are absolute, (non changing), they can experience all of time past present and future as revealed by God's spiritual power through His grace. As we live God's words according to His will, not our own, hereby we are connected to the body of Christ to experience all of Him through the eternal. Father, my God and my Lord in Christ Jesus from the Divine, that is to say from what is eternal, comes praises, song, dance and the tongue of the spoken language, are all to glorify You. Exhaltations are spiritual, rain as water vapor going up, they are collected in heaven. God blesses us as he keeps for his children the blessings to return in the latter rain, in spiritual life from the thanks givings that have gone forth. We have when we ask in the spiritual flow of Christ's righteousness inheritance of a rich heritage through the relationship with our living God. We've to let Christ live His life through us beholding God for who He is.

The Devil's kingdom has been destroyed by the power of the character of the blood of the lamb. Pure and perfect, innocent of transgression. My darkened mind has been shattered and now the light of the character of Jesus remains in the heat of the battle. Darkness is trying to cast doubt and fears, plant dark thoughts and distractions on every turn, within the senses of the flesh which scream out to the pains of birth. The process of being trained for righteousness is real, it is true. Be of good courage as it happens to you.

Oh Lord there are so many ways before me. I still do not consider you at all times, I need to be with the flow of your love. As I learn of you I'm put to death and must admit it to exchange for your life. When all else fails I plead your precious blood Lord and bathe in its unconditional forgiveness. God is with us, in us and we in Him, for those who call upon His name by grace forevermore. I have an allegiance to what is true though none go with me yet I must follow in order to live. The devil is a liar.

He tries to keep us from the love of God's presence. Through the sacrifice of Christ, the eternal spirit cleanses our consciousness and keeps them pure. No longer do we serve dead works, but now the King of life. It's the little things, not turned over to God, with every hit I'm taking from the friction, of my ways, I'm being ground into powder as they rob my life. I've got to be mindful, God is an ever present help in time of need when the pressures of life comes to squeeze, what comes out is going to produce life or death, "Help me my living God", or "I can handle it." God inhabits the praises of His people as they sing they enter into the reality of His presence and maintain it. **Beware** any friend of the world is an enemy of God. But love and pray for people, your enemy, don't judge them. **Beware** of people who have a cloak to shield themselves from the word of God and a hidden dagger to cut to defend their position. Who will justify their action even if they commit murder with blood on their hands, in their **eyes** they still have done no wrong. My relationship with God is contrary to the mindset of this world. My mind is sound and packed with righteousness, having order. My family and friends have come to me to question my sanity, but in the heat of their arguments, my mind is fixed to do the will of God. Just as Jesus said to Peter, "Get thee behind me Satan" and knew He had to die on the cross. I can taste the sweetness of my salvation, through grace, I have chosen not to partake of the spirit of this world, "what profit a man if he gains the whole world and he loses his only soul," for I have seen my destiny, my aim is for the mark of the high calling. I know where I'm going. Just as Moses turned from the pleasures of Egypt so turn I from bondage that goes along with these which please the flesh. I am a free man and no longer a slave, I lay down my life willingly and I give God all the glory, as He does reign as King over all the heavens and the earth. He broke the generational shackles of my chains with His own blood and cried out for me, "It is finished." Then He rose from the dead and took me with Him. To reign in glory by His side. I've been resurrected. I have tasted the divine, and I know now where I'm going to. Into the sheepfold as a defenseless lamb, and under my shepards protection, who is Jesus Christ. The Devil's head has been crushed and I'm not turning around to be turned to a pillar of salt the way Lot's wife did. I'm going forward forevermore, resting vulnerable and trusting in the grace of God.

When we have our direction, following to do the will of God, we should reflect the image of Christ. I rejoice my Heavenly Father, my delight is to do your will. Where life does reign through thanksgiving and song which comes from your Holy word. You've given me eyes of love to comprehend what I do in ignorance so that I can be forgiving and be salt and light in a darkened tasteless world. I've got to lay down my life in order to get life from above and take it up in His will. This allows me to become apart of His body, and experience eternal life. No longer to yield fruits of unrighteousness which lead to death, now that I'm out of the way there's room for God to work through me. I can recognize His voice, I now know what brings life and what brings death, I choose to live. There is no glory in the self, to pat myself on the back is death. Wrong motives, wrong actions, can make us sick. I'm determined to keep my vessel, by the grace of God, and follow Christ's actions. I'm learning how to do everything as unto the Lord for good health, in a spiritually unfriendly acting out world, which does not belong to us. That is why we're under attack and must fight to keep our faith to stay connected to where we belong from above. Eyes piercing the darkness in the night, shining light which seizes the wounds of the crevasses, cleaning the goo of decay from our minds and bringing life where death once ruled to take its toll. Jesus knows the way to life, after I tried all else, I now know Jesus is the way to life, therefore we should not exhibit a worldly character, "Vengeance is mine sayeth the Lord." I'll follow Him only! We are not of this world, just as Jesus is not of this world. He that is in me rejoices and I rejoice Jesus is in me. It is a fight to keep all my thoughts trained on Jesus as my mind is renewed, doing everything as unto the Lord, but to stay alive I must. Prayer, writing, reading the word of God, loving others, being thankful, praise and worship and encouraging one another in the faith have become essential. All our hopes, all our fears, all our memories from the past, God wants to wash over them, as we give them to Jesus, who restores to life that which the worm had eaten away. As my thought life is brought up from the past I watch as the worm wriggles and threads of light put out darkened deeds and continue to renew my mind.

> Lord Jesus whatever is mine
> shall be thine.
> I see your light through the midst of all my troubles
> Like the sun through gray clouds on a dismal day.
> All my thoughts that are trapped within my soul
> All that I possess which keeps me from being whole
> I believe, help thou my unbelief, that I may follow
> Even after the ends of the earth end
> your divine kingdom where your light breaks the dawn
> and cracks open all time, I believe, I believe, I believe
> whatever is mine shall be thine.
> Even though it's all already yours.
> Our lives are in a garden with weeds at every turn.
> They come in all shapes, sizes and colors, which bid us
> to come and attach ourselves to them. Then these weeds
> suck out our precious lives and we walk about as dead
> (did you ever hear someone say life sucks?)
> Jesus said "I am the resurrection."
> Life be!
> believe in me,
> though you were dead,
> yet shall you live.

Am I standing my ground, gaining ground, or losing my ground? The more of me I lose for Christ the more life I gain. What is my strategy to be? War plans of an invasion of love, actions of peace, words of encouragement. Visions of light eternal in Christ and yielded to the guidance into all truth of the Holy Ghost. We are islands, our thoughts, while beneath the surface of the water we're connected to the mountain of God. The sailboats which surround our islands are our emotions. By the islands we're at peace all is calm, where the trade winds blow. Storm winds catch our sails and we quickly lose sight of the islands and try to take control of situations on our own. We must not lose sight of the island or shipwreck is in store. No matter how dark storms may get or the fury of the winds that'll seem too strong for our vessels, or how dark the clouds of circumstance may get in our lives. Hold back, hold back I say, we've got to keep our emotions connected with our thoughts anchored soley on the word of God, to make it all the way through and back to the safety of our island ports.

If I talk without love, "I am become as sounding brass, or a tinkling symbol full of wind." <u>Destructive criticism</u> - sees something out of place and immediately tries to fix it without considering the other person's growth rate. It often tries to force its point of view in a condescending way, a quick fix to meet their needs which forces others to lie to their growth rate and deny their own identities. Do as I say or else, this brings division, pushes people away.

<u>Constructive criticism</u> - Identifies that the other person is not getting their needs met and encourages by walking along side, showing them examples as to why there's a better way to handle that situation or problem. This promotes an atmosphere where someone feels safe to try the other person's way and to grow back into order, without being forced against their will. People may be correct in their wanting something corrected but their procedure may be all wrong. We're here to help each other to learn how to grow better and not take a stance that could distance the ones we love when they may need our help the most. The Devil always tries to bring division. Love brings people closer together and to God.

<u>There's an importance to being thankful</u>, when someone receives the help or a gift from someone else and does not say thank you, they miss God's blessing and His presence. They'll feel they have something coming to them because they're in control of who they are, and are not vulnerable or sensitive to God. When someone says thank you this acknowledges there's forces outside themselves. This humbles themselves to a higher power which blesses where He finds His children seeking favors, with thanksgiving in their heart. Who are we thinking of when we say thank you? We are thanking God, through the spirit, and into eternity. God in return sends the blessing of knowing Him

which we receive as we partake of His divine nature bonding us to Himself as part of His character. True gratitude is a sign of health and being full of life. Ingratitude is a sign of being distanced in relationships and unhealthy with self esteem.

I believe there's a plain of existence with varying degrees of healthiness. Where depending on how close a child is raised to its parents, this will determine the type of choices which will be made in other relationships throughout their lives. Those who share the same reality live in the same world. Even after the body has died the spirit remains joined to the world it is connected. Either it can continue to be set in order, or put out of order with no rest. There are two spiritual flows. One moves us along all the time. The other flows through us when we are standing still and brings life, the other keeps us from it. Only what's built in Christ will last all other things are going to pass away from the presence of love and into torment where there is no love.

12

Under Attack

We have stored compartments of the past in our minds as we remember them, recall them, they bring illusions of life from the past which can block out our present. Interfere with a genuine faith which is what is real for building a sound mind. We've to rally all the troops (angels), through prayer and persevere to push out darkness from our minds and invite Christ's presence, His peace, fully into our realities that we may have an eternal perspective. Being wise as serpents and harmless as doves.

Don't let the Devil have its way with you. He wants to put out your light to sever your relationship with God. He will distract you with the cares of this world, in conversation we must be at peace to discern what is in the spirit of love and what is not. Be quick to pray and love, not to judge.

I go by the truth which is seen. The truth which is sewn into the fiber of my being, one strand of light at a time. This displaces all darkness and brings forth life wherever it shines, as water rolls off a duck's back so also sin off ours as we do the will of God. God invites us into His presence, His own personality, we see God and get to see our own true selves and what is not Him. We become content, our identity is with God and His ability to bring about change, which brings peace to otherwise troubled conditions. Even in the very midst of acting out Jesus is there saying, "come to me". Then we call upon Him, even afterwards always seeing He has the better way and our life is restored, the truth of Jesus changes things. We learn to see His ways first over our circumstances and this brings eternal life.

When we're around evil long enough it causes us to see that we don't belong there.

When we discover something in us that does not bring life we must grow out of it by pushing back the forces of darkness gradually leaving no ground for evil to regain lost or reopen territory, once the layers of light have been set in place without advancing ahead of ourselves. Peace and order is restored through the patience with our Lord and Savior Jesus Christ, to Him to work all things in us as we grow. One line of light at a time, till we're rooted and grounded in the word of God. We must endure all things until one person comes into focus in every area of our lives, Jesus Christ. The eye shifts, we lose sight of the task at hand, then finding our way back to thoughts of righteousness become a struggle, as we lose our way on an errand of our King. A thread of light holds our sight as long as we hold on. All else is darkness till our eyes remember and see the light and resume our way again. I have no life outside of Christ, I'm a living stone who follows commands as a part of His body.

I can see the darkness all around, the blind are leading the blind and are growing darker still, I pray for them for as so once was I. Got to keep my eyes on the light for the battle is never over. In the heat of any moment, a test, when things are not going our way. We're to be still, look through to the outcome, as to it's end result life or death. It is only when this picture is not complete our emotions detach from our thoughts and we try to handle things in our own strength. We neglect to consider God's ways above our own, "our very strength, life and breath."

The eyes from the sky are mine looking back at me as His words are alive in me, and I alive in Jesus, I can see I see through His spirit. We try to obtain and we have not and that which we do have gets taken away. God's power is available to us, which is greater than sin, to overcome any evil in the heat of temptation. Other people are going to test our realities just to see how genuine we are. We must be at rest with God's spirit moving us continually, throughout our day. To pass the test we're to have an unmovable reality of the Eternal, which was opened to us at the cross, resting in the finished work of Jesus Christ, death defeated.

Visions are shared with other people. When I see Jesus and there's no one else to share it with, then my identity becomes challenged. If I'm the only one who thinks the way I do, then it suggests that there's something wrong with me. However, if my reality aligns itself with truth constant, then even though I stand alone, the truth bares witness of itself and I remain sane, even if the rest of the world is off balance and does not agree with the true reality of God. When people don't recognize our authority, our love from God, they're not going to listen to us, for they are focussed on this off balanced world's spiritual system.

If we eat fruit before it ripens it has no or little taste and is hard to eat. I can't pick this fruit from the tree and try to force it on others to eat. I must let it ripen and fall off on its own. Now that Christ redeemed us we start to see what's lacking in others and are able to reach out in love as we now have life as sweet fruit to offer, to give in turn as we're now who Jesus says we're to be, (in Him).

Authority must be sincerely loving, genuinely supportive, gentle and patient if its going to be heard. To wait and pray is needed for us to see how we fall short (not reflecting God's character), and for God to bring ourselves and others perceptions to His reality. It's important to send God first, before our struggles, to admit to ourselves He is greater than I and prove eternity is the place all time belongs to God. It is here transference of realities occurs, from the Devil's kingdom of death and darkness to God's kingdom of eternal light and life, where we desire to do God's will and live. "Jesus has overcome the world."

When time is ours if left alone, to our own ways, without having our identities reinforced from the eternal, then our needs become warped. We reach outwardly at all costs to have our needs met. Even if it means risk to a gentle character that may damage itself to the point where it gets abused and has its life reconditioned on a downward spiral warp after warp to its own destruction.

I remember as a child coming to a stage in my growth where I went from following choices to making them. At this stage, looking back, fears came to me in the night when I tried to go to sleep. I now can see there were forces that tried to influence my thinking (through power of creation), at this time of enchantment when the business of the day and my thoughts became unveiled they'd try to eat my life away. These fears came as a result of being set up for a warped perception. A denied reality minus direction leads to a pool of confusion where damage takes place.

I'm angry and my anger is coming from the neglect I experienced as a child. A lack of love, nurturing, gave me unhealthy needs which led to dark choices. I have three of my own children (on loan from God), and know their needs; mine had to have been known of, people just looked blindly on or the selfish other way. Oh Lord, I grieve for the small boy who needed attention to grow in the right direction, to find light in a darkened world. I embrace that small boy and welcome him into the light, and draw him close to the word of God in me, which gives life to me as I yield my will to the Father the way Jesus does, through His grace.

I'm no longer to be part of the curse which separates from life. Jesus is in me and I in Him. I choose to receive His light and love, let US move as ONE, forevermore, forward in the truth of Your word. With Jesus at the center of everything we do, spontaneity should come through His eyes looking back at us.

I see the world is sick because people choose to live outside of God's light. They prefer the off balance chaos, disease, blind madness rather than the ray of God's light which heals and makes known the way to go for life. I understand we're to forgive others, who in their ignorance put us to death daily, as we see them worshipping false gods which keeps them in the condition they're in.

By rejecting the true and living God they keep bleeding, unaware as to the final destruction that awaits them: separation from God for eternity and its torments.

An Example of This is Shown In My A Vision of Hell. Take a complainer and he'll complain throughout eternity, not wanting to complain, and with each empty complaint he'll get less and less satisfaction and they'll be no one to complain to. This holds true for sex, neurosis, impatience, anger, uneasiness, never enough in all areas of emotional pains, simultaneously, with ever-increasing tendencies to not be able to express yourself and a sense of being ground down (chewed) to greater and greater depths of despair without hope. People will be able to call on their own gods, things from the world, they knew them and be tormented even more when getting no response. They'll get no revelation that will bring them to a point of salvation. All the fears, worries, cares, etc of this world will be there only it will get worse and worse and worse. In addition, they'll have other spirits of the unseen realm which torment with even more suffering. Anything that Satan tricked man into trying to lift up and exhalt himself with in the presence of Holy almighty powerful glory of God, will burn them throughout eternity. The Glory light of God will burn lost souls, who know not Christ the one and only savior, to such a degree they'll have no choice but to flee His presence and be consumed in pain, knowing they can never have this glorious love all the while. A land where all the nightmares come to life and there's no way to wake up. No light to pierce the darkness to redeem and change for new life, all is lost, all is lost, all is lost.

When we listen to God and obey to not give in to the lusts of the flesh, we grow. If we do not let go of the things of the world it is impossible to grow on with Him. The only way to let go is to ask Him to take them from a stand still position. God walks us through by carrying us to safety. He lays us down in Eternal life, only we've got to learn to abide and to be mindful not to go from His presence.

Everyone does something for a reason, there's no such thing as chance. All our actions can be traced to original motives which are set into action by spirits to manipulate us and steal our lives while unaware. We must trace our steps and see what puts our lives into motion. What is the source of energy which motivates us, Love + Truth = Light or Lies + Hate = Darkness?

It is the resurrection power of Christ in every area of our lives which cause us to arise from death unto life. When a spirit invades our mind it tries to get us to denounce Christ and take over, to possess us. When we realize God's life has gone out of us we must call upon Him, to be reestablished in a relationship. Then allow God to push out the evil spirits, heal the tear in our soul, and fill us with His presence, thus walk in newness of life, separated from the spirits of this world. We're not to imitate the things of this world for they have no life in them. We are to only reflect the image of the creator, worshipping Him, and not the creature.

The mind is a map. We must be careful what we draw on it with our thoughts. These thoughts lead us into the eternal with God's consciousness or stranded in darkness with no way of escape. It is important to be honest map readers and recognize God's conscience which will direct us around every turn. If I misstep waiting for help to come can be difficult. For dark choices come knocking at our door, to leave our position of safety, a trust in thee living God. We must refuse all dark calling thoughts the moment we see them or it could mean our very life. God wants us to ask of Him that our joy may be full.

If we lose our eternal vision be mindful to remember the character of Christ, His truth constant word. Then when God moves we'll move and when He is still, we'll be still as well. God with His spirit builds according to His own time table. If something gives us a pretense of order and tries to accelerate the eternal reality of God's super natural work, then it will be accursed in the long run. Like a tree toppling over for lack of root, no good thing will come of it. Learning when to move and when not to move takes complete discipline. We don't realize things that have our affections in this world are the things which may be killing us. Prayer without ceasing, meditating on God's word day and night, encouraging one another in the faith, praise and worship in song, with our actions and our words being thankful for the eternal reality of God must all come together as a part of His grace, to train the mind in righteous behavior. We are to move on this path of life, the way a train gets pulled by electricity along the third rail. We get pulled along by spiritual forces of our own choosing, through the tongue we draw through spoken words and our actions. These in turn determine what track we're on. Righteousness or unrighteousness to fill us with life or death as we move along. This discipline will change us by causing us to defend our position with what we see in our mind's eye. The eternal reality of God or our own darkened understanding mind.

I will not give in to another identity as long as I know the one I follow now has life and allows me to be true to who I am. I choose to kiss the truth and live, no matter what heat from the friction I experience of others who go against my choice to follow may be. Your Eternal reality my Lord Jesus, it is by grace I know I'm to be your King's man and reflect your character at any cost. Thank you for your reality to carry it out as I learn of you along the way a little more each and every day.

Lord as I embrace you I experience your life, my breath becomes your breath, your spirit flowing through me, there's nowhere else to go but to you. A house may fully be renovated but the reality must be changed for the spirit of God to move in and bring eternal life. Come and meet Him who opens the eyes of the blind and raises the dead, who is the door to the Eternal way. My eyes are fixed, continue to guide me in your word by your spirit. So skillful and gentle is your touch, the truth never misses its mark, I'll know no other but you, amen.

Jesus always says follow me, then it's up to us to follow or not. Whenever eyes meet worlds touch. For protection we're to look through to Jesus our rock, sword and shield and be at peace in His light. I've had people attack me with what they think I need, with the best of intentions. For it appears to people with worldly minds, I'm lacking. My Lord is all I need attacks others realities, what's wrong with you that you're not like us. They make me the troubled one to reinforce their own darkened identities. Jesus said, "If a man keeps my words he will never taste death." The world tries to discredit what God's word promises for they don't want to admit they're eating death. I've tasted life eternal and I'm not going to eat death anymore! Be careful, the Devil wants us to join their lie, to lie to ourselves and become as them, making us no longer a threat to their ways. We're to pass through the midst of them the way Jesus did when His life was threatened by stoning after speaking the truth and having it rejected in the synagogues.

All my thoughts were dark, then they fought against the light. Now my thoughts are light and they fight against the dark, my mind's recovered right before my eyes. I hold my ground and am confident in what I know. I've seen mountains a far off in the distance and even in the present, past, future be removed and cast into the sea. My testimony, peace now stands where chaos once ruled. I've learned to be still in God's love and allow Him to fight my battles. All the while being patient, every day with faith, knowing God is on the move, my promises are yea and amen.

Beware of serpents that lay wait in shadowy places in others, who stray from the light of God, rejecting His word and spirit, even though they profess to know Him.

Beware of sitting in the judgement seat. A place where you will not receive the blessings of God. It is not possible to give thanks or worship unless you're looking at Him.

The tongue is a sword which swings both towards and away from us. If we swing a dark sword death will enter us and move towards others. A light sword will counter with life and build righteous character, use your sword well remembering to keep it pure.

God works with potential, not with what is. He loves us and gives us free will never forcing us to obey Him, even when we may harm ourselves. We must first see eternal light, or hear His voice, in order to respond to God, then discover His better way, and then turn over the control of our life. My children helped to teach me the need for a better way full time. I know to do battle in my strength means spiritual death. Lord Jesus, I know you've called me now, here I am, send me standing still.

13

Treasure Chest

Forgive me Father I failed. I thought I'd put myself to rest, but when my anger exceeded my patients instead of calling on you, I tried to handle the situation with my own strength. I read the map in my mind and saw someone else's criteria other than yours Lord Jesus. 1 John 5:5 Who is he that overcometh the world, but he that believeth that Jesus is the son of God. Thank you Jesus for forgiving me with your precious blood. For your cleansing, your healing and for your restoration of life and my King's honor all made new again. As though I'd never gone astray, my treasures once again are returned not to be ignored. Lord keep me mindful to cry out to you in time of need that I may grow to be kept from error. 1 John 5:18 "We know that whosoever is born of God sinneth not; but he that is begotten of God keepeth himself, and that the wicked one toucheth him not."

Lord I need to worship you more. I need to cry out till I enter into the attitude of living righteously, that when I turn around to look back on my life I see You standing there. Then I want to shed my earthly body, Lord I'm groaning in my spirit to enter into the place where I reach your throne. I see now, then what will be next? "The just shall live by faith." Your touch doth revive my soul, thank you Jesus for saving my soul from darkness which had encamped round about me, You pulled me out and set me up upon your rock that is higher than I and now I will praise thee all the day long. My God doth hear the cries of His people.

When we get overwhelmed in life, we need to empty ourselves before God the way Jesus did that we may be filled also. Mat 4:4 it is written, man shall not live by bread alone, but by every word that proceeded out of the mouth of God. Fill me with your word Lord God and give discernment by your spirit that there will be life. When walls close in on all sides without hope, I'll remember your word then Jesus will take me up above. We need to go down lower, as low as our knees in prayer and refuse the world, its kingdom powers and riches, the devil offers and his lie to worship him by using our strength trying to get us to deny the reality of God. By allowing God to love me I can serve Him best. "Whosoever shall not receive the Kingdom of God as a little child shall not enter therein." This opens the door for us to be in God's Kingdom of truth His word and press on with a density of trust in our living Lord. When the enemy comes in like a flood to wash us away, God raises up a standard for the way to go by His word. Then is there life where there was no life before. Wait, watch and maintain conscience contact with the living God. As God doth breathe by His word with His continual love burning towards us, we can see the way to go, Love + Truth = Light, which yields "seek peace and pursue it." Jesus is the prince of peace. I now thank Him daily, for saving me, especially when the taste of love isn't in my mouth, then I'm renewed.

> Our creator who is above and before all others we are in a relationship with You
> You have a holy and pure character, You are order.
> We've a growing building relationship with You, drawing closer, knowing more of You, and gaining understanding Trusting Your ways as better than our own the same way we relate to Your will in time on earth will be the same way as in eternity.
> A touch of Your presence in our relationship with You is needed to maintain a continual conscious contact as life and take all barriers away which block our relationship with You keep ourselves open to let Your love flow through us to others let nothing come between us as to be unseperable Keep my mind pure and in touch with eternal life at all times the way You govern will last forever with invincible reign beyond the conditions of time. Amen.

When we dive into the water we enter into another reality and it takes us time to adjust, finally we come up for air. In the reality of the eternal we're able to swim about and move, breath and be full of life without any temporal behaviors to clog us up by bringing disorder to disrupt our conscience contact with thee Eternal Flame our loving God.

Without an understanding of how an ongoing relationship with God works is like having a bull in a china shop. Unfortunately you're the china shop without any directions on how to get the bull out. Jesus make me aware of any bulls I still have roaming around, that I may ask you to remove them, in your wisdom, with your love, amen.

Mixed messages send confusing signals. When someone says I love you and lies or acts out as our realities are being shaped we're going to equate love as having these characteristic defects.

Love + Lies + Truth = inconsistencies which blind us as to what is the true direction for life. Jesus knows Love + Truth perfected, this sheds light for the correct direction to follow, and He sits in eternity holding open the door to life.

We find His path when we grow weary of the jumbles of Hate + Lies + Truth or Love and Hate + Truth have wearied us to the point of crying out for help, "save me!" Then we're ready to follow.

Jesus came to serve not to be served. As the Holy Spirit leads us into all truth we sense God's love in our relationship with Him. If we behave in a way which is contrary to God's truth or love we break ties with Him and lose our way. If we are to have a close walk with God, we need a mind filled with God's truth and a body filled with His love, which cannot happen if sin is in the way. Order puts what's out of order in order in an orderly way; this is the only way to life. Psalm 19:14 let the words of my mouth and the meditation of my heart, be acceptable in thy sight, Oh Lord, my strength and my redeemer.

We can't help anyone else unless we are set in order, Jesus knows this, He remains in order so others can follow and be set in order. It's easy to look at others, but in doing so, we take our eyes from God and lose the order of our way in the process.

"Broad is the road to destruction, narrow is the road to salvation." When we have eternity in our eyes we'll speak the language of wisdom and righteous judgement to sustain order in the vision of following Jesus to keep our life, and the way to it.

When we stray and leave God's will we're going to experience discomfort until we return again to God's leading. I want you to know there are mountains and valleys in our walk with God. When we're in the light as He is in the light we can see where we are going and receive the blessings of God. At the top of the mountain there's no known problems, our eyes are on the will of God and we can trust what we can see as unified. Matt. 5:14 Ye are the light of the world. A city that is set on a hill cannot be hid.

However, we enter valleys when God speaks to us about our sin and we get stubborn, then disobedient, or even rebellious which turns us away from the will of God. It is a device of darkness to get us to feel guilty as to keep us from bonding with the light of God's love again. Your relationship will grow again, be patient. Wait on the Lord and gain experience. Warning just because you've seen something off in the distant future doesn't mean you've grown there yet, remember your balance. Rejoice in the hope of the glory of God and have faith God will bring you all the way through, loving you all the while in His time. Peter denied Jesus three times in one day, as foretold by Jesus, "Before the rooster crows twice you, Peter, shall deny me thrice."

Peter must of found himself in a dark valley where he lost sight of God. In these valleys the devil comes and attacks us with voices of discouragement as well, while we're in the dark he is there also, and he speaks to our thoughts, trying to attach Himself to us in the sight of God, now listen in. "If I just look the other way this once, it'll be alright," "I'm so depressed I'm gonna kill myself," "I'm all alone and nobody loves me." Then there are the voices of rejection. "I've been told I'm not worth anything," "After all that effort I'm a big zero," "They don't accept Jesus the way I always shared Him anymore," "You're not welcome here anymore go find somewhere else to live," "I trusted and now the disappointment hurts, oh so bad."

Circumstance can overwhelm us too. "I've lost my job," "My wife wants a divorce," "My kids are on drugs," "My daughter is pregnant," "I stubbed my toe again," "I cut myself," "The rent is due and I haven't the money, fire, car accidents." How we handle these situations can cause us to climb out or sink lower into the valley, we're being sanctified all the while. I also want to make mention of some of the voices of pride. "I'm gonna take care of number one," "The hell with everybody else I count, too, don't I?," "Well, if they're gonna be that way I'll get even," "Fine, if that's the way you want it, you got it," "I can't take all this pressure," "I'm gonna kill myself." Are we steadfast in love with Christ? It is in the valleys where our faith gets tested the most. The devil wants us to break our faith with God and focus on the issues of life rather than where life comes from, putting fear in faith's place.

Upon experiencing something eternally new, a light from the mountain to lead the way, there's a stage of transition which occurs. During this processing clarification takes place. We gain understanding and comprehend, as in the case where one of my daughters teased her sister till she stopped responding, she in turn stopped acting out and ceased teasing thus becoming versatile to the stimuli at hand. Through expressions of trials we put off what is false to obtain what is real, or build on what is presently true, to enhance more growth for life.

I see now there's a spirit behind the anger and rage in me which rises up and tries to take control when I try to handle situations in my own strength. We've got to learn to defend ourselves with God's word and expose these spirits or we won't last. By spotting these spirits that tag along and identifying them we learn what to ask of the Lord as we turn to Him instead of the spirits. These masks get pulled off one after the other, till the one that is left is really ours, which should reflect the light of Christ. All of our clothing must come off as well till we're naked, vulnerable before ravenous wolves, and do nothing to defend ourselves when the heat is on. We're to stand and not let down our shields so we may have light in the face of adversity. We're to love Jesus in us more than our fleshy selves and be kept in the fire of God's all-consuming flame, not burned as in the case of the devil's demonic forces.

If we move out of sync with God we're open to attack when we're not by His side. The devil wants us to go out in our own strength to be like him and fall. He wants to steal our life because he doesn't have any of his own, being separated from God himself. By grace God comes, when we cry out for help, He picks us up and holds us till we recognize His way once again. We must be filled continually, having fellowship with God, to have life. The devil runs from this light of God's as to avoid being removed.

When he's exposed we can see the ugliness of our way and flee from it, which causes the devil to lose his hold on us. Thus we find our way to freedom and out of another valley. Ephesians 6:12. "We wrestle not against flesh and blood, but against principalities, against powers, against the rulers of the darkness of this world, against spiritual wickedness in high places."

We enter valleys when we are tempted and drawn away by our own desires. Enticed into a promise which appears as life to our flesh, but the end result takes us off the path of following Jesus Christ, which means death to our spiritual life. "There are many ways that seem right to a man but the end result is death." "Every perfect gift is from above 'the mountain tops,' and cometh down from the father of lights, with whom there's no variables, neither shadow of turning."

"But as it is written, eye has not seen, nor ear heard, neither have entered into the heart of man, the things which God hath prepared for them that love Him." Love draws people closer to God, the self pushes people further away, it is His spirit which trains us to know the difference. Only then can we see where we're going. Without the word of God our mindseye remains dull. I'm not going to lose ground, I'm going to love and forgive the way Jesus does. My delight is to will to do the will of the Lord where there's light and life forever more. As we partake of the divine nature of God, God partakes of it with us, bonding Himself to ourselves. If we find ourselves in indecision, at a crossroad for a choice of direction to take, be still, wait on the

Lord, call upon Him. Our peace will be restored when we know our blessings will not get in the way of the blesser.

The words of the bible are alive and have my fondest affections. As does those who live by the word as well. Serving God should give us a center of joy, from the ease of His load, with contentment. Serving ourselves gives us a center of headaches from the weight of our load and the order we try to maintain, while keeping it.

First the seed, the shoot, the stem, then budding branches to the budding flowers. Year upon year till at last the fruit. Things take time to grow. It takes time for people to realize the righteousness of Christ in them and follow it. First they have to be allowed to discover they have a need for it, after they realize they're tasting death, they know of the need for life and become weary of unrighteousness. Honor with thanksgiving allows the spirit of God to fill us and reflect His character. The spirit of God comes upon us and remains that we may carry out His will, as long as we do not quench His spirit by turning away and land in a valley.

Joy is produced through a conscience awareness of grace. God blesses through grace. Him laying down His life, love, truth, light, understanding, peace and entering into His promises, for us, through perseverance are all apart of grace. I follow after Jesus because He knows what I do not know about life and I know it and love Him for it. He alone gives revelation knowledge and makes known the way of life. The gift of Christmas is the birth of eternal life. "His resurrection blasts the way to eternity that we may follow His life," your gift forevermore. Everyday is Christmas for those who believe, fore eternal life has no death, fore time has been cracked open. Celebrate! His loving you.

As we walk through the world we gather dust. If we don't bring our dirt to God when the winds blow of tribulations it becomes a storm and we lose our way, the dust is always settling. We must bring our needs to the Lord and stop dealing with them on our own, or the weight of them will become a burden that will crush us to death. As a vessel of honor full of light in a darkened world I am apart of the body of Jesus Christ.

I will magnify the Lord giving Him the glory and praise. The closer I get to Christ the fewer people seem to stick around, but some do come back when they realize there's no where else to go as I've learned. I pray, Jesus be my strength, be my sanity in an insane world where people slip away into shadows from your light. Be order where order does not exist so that my life will be sustained, kept as creation in the midst of a dark void. I am revived, my spirit has been renewed.

Either God is God or man is God. "Jesus humbled Himself to be a man and do the Father's will, not to exhalt His authority above it." He obeyed as the light of the world, knowing all, fore he knew our darkened conditions. He further humbled Himself to shed light, with the truth of His love, into us to meet our needs out of compassion. We must focus on this reality and see the train of our thoughts. Where are they taking us? Then be objective as to what we're to see, do we want to stay on our train of thoughts, or get off and go somewhere else?

I see a storm coming and we need to be ready. Destruction is at the door, senses are not going to last and what is pleasing to them passes away from moment to moment. The things of the spirit last forever and do not change. People get driven to distraction and go blind as to see what is happening to them, for they've been seduced by the flesh. They miss the spirit of God within plain sight and die for the lack of knowledge.

The Father's seed in Mary, Jesus grew up obeying the Father. The Father's seed in us through Jesus, now we too can obey the Father of Heaven, and not the Father of this world, the Devil. "People get so wrapped up in their own things that when trouble comes they can't find God," for all they have is their own devices to fall back on and see only their own sorrows.

Thou art in me Lord Jesus and I in thee. Lord I'm not always going to say or do the right thing, keep me humble enough to admit it. Lord, I want to be your servant and no one else's. I surrender my vision to you, Lord Jesus. Work it in me cause I'm not able to go there, I'll wait on you, help me grow there. I don't have any trouble when I see beyond the mountains, all I need is faith in the living God.

I must wait for my children to cry out for help, the way God waits for me. If God does not open my mouth (with love and truth), it does not pay to speak for it's only going to bring death.

> Gonna start a fire now
> By praising the living Lord
> I will wait upon His name
> and cause friction with His word
> my coals are red and kindled
> As His wind starts a-blowin'
> The sparks are jumping now
> Then the flames leap about
> His fire is coming, it can't be contained
> The Lord's fire is here and it's gonna spread
> Cause I'm a gonna shout it out
> and dance in the all-consuming flames
> not to be burned in His presence
> The almighty God my maker
> Master and Savior Jesus Christ
> My King of glory and Lord of everything.

I must lose my life to gain eternal life. Once Jesus' light of truth shines and He speaks to us, we've no cloak for our sins. We either repent, or go away from His light into darkness; however there's always grace to ask God for help. Part of which involves making things harder for us when we disobey to get our attention. The Lord chastens those who he loves, so they'll cry out to Him for help and return to His spirit of life. However, returning to God we expect Him to accept us, only we don't realize we want to bring our flesh along before God. When following Jesus Christ we try to justify, through grace, our worldly pleasures of darkness to feel comfortable about having our spiritual lives sucked out of us, like water going down a drain. When Christ is our only sacrifice we are possessed with things which lead to an eternal relationship and have no time for earthly pleasures which no longer satisfy the spirit. In place of the flesh we're filled to crying out for God's direction, His will, His life and singing praise to worship and adore Him all the day long. We're on fire and are proud to burn with humility anytime, in front of anybody, and any place Jesus would have us to burn. This is where grace leads to, "count the cost take up your cross and follow Him." Romans 8:1. "There is therefore now no condemnation to those who are in Christ Jesus, who does not walk according to the flesh, but according to the spirit, 'which brings life.'" Paul also said, "I labored more than all of them, yet not I but the grace of God that worketh in me." As we yield too we're also not aware of our service. God in our hands, our hands in God.

You can't teach someone of themselves, or the message they bare, if they're living their lives through darkened influences which surround them. Wearing blinders they are trained to look in a temporal direction which makes it difficult for them to experience the eternal. They don't know their temples are filled with death and their own thoughts cannot be trusted for life. Col. 3:2. Set your affections on things above, not on things of the earth. Rom. 20

And the God of peace shall bruise Satan under your feet shortly. I must go forth in prayer to maintain conscience contact with God to push back all darkened mindfulness and be protected by God. Rom. 8:16. The spirit itself beareth witness with our spirit, that we are the children of God. God's word is a miracle. There are those who laugh at the resurrection of Jesus, yet here I am with eternal life in my veins to prove them wrong and everything about the bible true. Even though I walk alone most of the time, I know the way to life and whoever sees my life, it is my prayer they are joined to Jesus as well. Our moves are always being watched as is our words.

After each battle as joy comes in and there's a tendency to let down our guard. Then the devil comes to us and says, "Look how great you're doing, pamper yourself." He wants to attach his spirit to our flesh and get us to focus on ourselves to get a foot hold. Also remember the joy of the Lord is our strength and as we abide in Jesus, there's no place for the devil. Wait on the Lord and be strengthened, call upon Him and He will answer you.

If our character strays from the truth so will all those who hold us in high esteem. Acknowledging the presence of God must take place when we pray, or as we live. There's a still, quiet voice, when we too are still, the meek do inherit the earth without giving their life (the spirit of God), away, rather they share it instead.

Never try to get approval from people who have worldly characters, who live for the approval of each other and go into a darker pit. They beat things into order with their own strength and exhaust their energy. When time is ours we survive and manipulate circumstances and things to fit our own order, we become a god. When something is out of place our whole balance is disrupted and our world becomes chaos, we run on feeling empty with trying to fill in the missing piece continually lacking order and fight convinced it's the only way.

When time belongs to God we live life. God's in control and He maintains order with His strength. The friction of time is laid to rest and we experience the eternal, we are filled in. With focus off of selfish needs we're free to enjoy life in the spirit and overcome the lusts of flesh.

We are born into a spiritual death separated from God, who calls to us, "Come, surrender to me and I'll take care of you." For loss of words at crucial moments. I see between the lines and cannot answer. How do you explain to an infant what it cannot understand? (We must pray and wait for God to teach them.) When questioned about desires which still have my flesh I must confess, "I'm waiting to see what Jesus will do." Then patiently watch Him work with love until I understand. Jesus (God's living word), gives clear perception to live on His path of order, and be born into the eternal. Where life takes death's place and we become connected to God. I find substance here. All I have and all I do, at my best, I surrender to God's working in me.

Spending to carry out the work of God is exciting and joyous. We're called to be good stewards on how we spend ourselves and our substance, or we won't reap the fullness of life God has to offer.

It's been my observation that people are generally too busy to hear or see the truth and make excuses to avoid it. Their minds are not open to the eternal's movements. They travel the desert dry and parched, when just a scratch beneath the sand or a simple word to a rock, will bring living waters to quench their thirst and give abundant life. Other people seek life and miss unless they connect during observations as to what be lie or truth. Ps. 56:13 For thou hast delivered my soul from death: wilt not thou deliver my feet from falling, that I may walk before God in the light of the living? Unfortunately people don't know they can cry out to the living God for true direction. Instead they return to a life of falsehood and go nowhere. They are filled with ways not becoming to them, which although seem safe they retain no life or honor, and cause friction with all those who are in their way. This friction starts at birth, then comes the struggle for help, babies cry out in faith that their needs will be met. They're looking to return to the order of the womb, its security, its safety and that God is going to take them there.

It is my observation young children are cared for and make very few decisions for themselves. They're told what to do, when to, where to and how to dress, eat, play, sleep, etc. As they get older and start to make more decisions, their trust for their parents' care for them must be transferred to God is going to care for them now. And lead them in the decisions they're going to make, to keep them connected to the womb's experience, trusting God to bring them through life. When Jesus said suffer the little children to come unto me. He didn't push them away, when drawing boundaries we must take care as not to reject our children, remembering what we reflect will affect them throughout their lives and the people they connect with.

Children act out to escape from the pain of insecurities of their decision-making process which has not been turned over to the control of God through His reflections in others. If children are lead to believe they can trust themselves without consulting God, then they'll inherit darkness and all the risks, fears, insecurities and disorder that go along with it. Rather than the confidence of the light, which comes from loving the truth, to obtain direction and understand plain sight.

114

It is important to me I share what I write as proof that the words of Jesus and His spirit are indeed alive in me, and I in Him. We are all on a quest to regain our lives to maintain where truth + love = light will take us. By God's saving grace the beads of truth have come together. I find there's enough new life in me now to say I've been restored. I believe eternal truth living in us is the only true reality for life everlasting. I've experienced both joys and sorrows along this path. I meet and depart from other saints, growing warm in love, to fulfill the purpose. We must stay faithful in our callings if we're to sharpen each other in Christ. We'll then put out darkness beneath our feet as we climb higher, still higher and in the end we'll all be together in glory. Where knowing Jesus will continue forevermore but for now one day at a time. Rev 22: 14, 15, 17. Blessed are those who do His commandments, that they may have the right to the tree of life and may enter into the gates through the city. But outside are dogs and sorcerers and sexually immoral and murderers and idolaters, and whoever loves and practices a lie. And the spirit and the bride say, "Come!" And let him who hears say, "Come!" And let him who thirsts come. Whoever desires let him take of the waters of life freely.

There's room at the table (truth constant), come and dine.

14

The Gift

We recognize the gift of salvation as it comes when we hold so dear to its freedom, above our own merited mindset, trusting God to bring it to pass. We take on the identity, words and actions of Jesus Christ. His birth, we start to understand the word of God and grow in stature and wisdom as we rely on the Holy Spirit for support more than our divisive structures. His ministry, standing firm against everything that does not seek to do Abah Father's will believing the promises of God and His word more than the reality of time, over lies leading to misperceptions, as to what the actuality of what life really is. Reaching out to others who are hurting who are still in the shoes you've just stepped out of; in Christs timing, through His grace. The cross, being willing to die for the direction of what I believe, knowing there's no other way to go, even if I wanted to. Dead and buried, living with the decision I made, having a clear conscience, above what the outcome has been for me, resting in judgement by grace with a complete trust God keeps the promise of His word. Resurrection, experiencing the reality of eternal order raised over the out of order unreality of time.

Thank you for going before me Lord Jesus my King, now I too may know the way. Knowing you've suffered all the steps before mine, drives me forward through the pain of unreality which I'm so often encumbered with as your spirit of life 'lovingly' takes the place of my man of death. You are the way, the truth and the life. No man comes to the Father but by you. Jesus my mighty warrior, thy kingdom come, thine will be done in the earth as it is in heaven. The battle is to keep the reality of Jesus Christ, the eternal flame alive, through faith justified. I surrender. Lord be my _____ at this time of need. God has made provision through His son to be joined to Himself throughout the day. I'm learning to lean on Jesus and depend upon His cleansing and keeping word. His life before me and all the misperceptions of the world behind. My focus to press on through all the unrealitys of time as I step in line with the Master and into His riches, honor, and glory as we become one, fore God is one in truth + love = light. We are the truth of God through the knowledge of His word by faith and where the unconditional acceptance of this love meet, it is here where revelation light allows us to gain access into oneness with Eternal God.

Being holy I pass through things which are unholy, standing still I'm freed up of self I'm teachable now and can experience more abundant life. Just as long as my spirit man is in control being joined to God, not the man of flesh joined to world and things there of which are passing away. I'm under such heavy attack as I hear the whispers from the world calling to my flesh. I cry out Lord I need you to be my all and all as I pass over from death unto life. To know your many names of provision to cover all my vulnerabilities, Jesus I'm open to attack. I need the complete order of Your love + truth = light as I orbit around you for my very life. We all are in orbit as we draw and are held according to our convictions. There be forces that attempt to pull us out of an orderly orbit and into a destructive one.

Take aim, keeping your eyes fixed on what is before not behind. Like a bullet the resurrection power of God, through the faith barrel, we're fired towards the target of sanctification. Every motion forward replaces the passing of time with the reality of God's word for the present. Whenever God bows down the heavens, and comes down putting the darkness of time under His feet, as in psalm 18:9, there's a release of power creating a bridge which penetrates the world of sin and death, darkness and the devil, unto light, the Kingdom of the heavenly Father and the gift of Eternal life. God loves us so much, He takes time out to come when we call. The end result of salvation's gift is in knowing the peace of God which it produces yielding a relationship with God, furthering our knowledge of our grace, which causes us to rejoice.

In God's domain eternity is unlimited with a solid core of love and truth combined to form the word of God equaling light, equaling Jesus. When our focus, love and truth, becomes life with a Christ center, we are put into an orbit through our convictions which yields to what we'll relate to. The same way the earth promotes life in its perfect orbit, by God's grace, around the sun, too close we'd burn, too far we'd freeze. We need to maintain an orbit around God which promotes a relationship with Him in which we can grow the best.

There are depths, widths, heights and breadths to God's eternal reality making it three dimensional. The more we learn of God the larger the cube of His life gets in an orderly uniform expansion of His reflection which lifts us from the limits of times dimension saving us.

In time, orbits are flat. They don't last long for when they try to expand there's no bonding to what is eternal, only to what is temporary. They slide by to repeat the cycle with no escape from the pains of death which give a distaste for life. You can't add limitations together, dysfunction never leads to the best possible choice, there's no sight for life with spontaneous behavior which acts out without considering its base or point of origin. There's no room to build or grow as all is stifled when hate combines with lies to put darkness at its center. There's no light for convictions and no sight of conditions which allows lies, truths, love, hate combined to create death on an orbit to destruction. The center we orbit around and how we apply it in our daily lives gives us the benefits of what we partake of or the lack there of. Do we call on Jesus throughout the day or by our silence do we pass by and get damaged.

In three dimensional sight the full scope of God is open to life to be enjoyed to the fullest as He meets all our needs as we cry out for help. God is at the center of life, from Him all blessings flow. One dimensional living is filled with elusive lies that keep us flat, we orbit around self and its limits. We conjure up things to amuse us to be occupied from moment to moment, there's always a need to control what we allow into our center for we are our own god. "What profit a man if he gain the whole world and lose his only soul?" Making and keeping conscience contact with God, in a relationship which grows into a better, fuller, enhancement of life, we experience a gradual transfer from a one to a three dimensional living which replaces sin with eternal life after salvation.

An emergence takes place as we're born into a Christ-centered lifestyle, with God a three dimensional person teaching us how to be 3D people in a flat, lost, ungodly world. We've to be true to who we are in Christ, even though we can only see Him through His word, we're not to serve our one dimensional fleshly selves. Now I'm to be still being aware I'm in a hostile time dimension, calling out with my new eternal tongue, to the Lord Jesus in His dimension, entering in expanding as I grow. Abiding in the vine I receive His eternal life continually, to meet all of the need for what His will is for me, which is better than times best choices are. Our relationship with Christ, the bride as to the groom we yearn for each other. Should the bride get jitters and go her own way Jesus comes again, as He appeared unto His disciples when He rose again, He appears unto us with His presence to renew our faith. This direction is the finish line, Christ the author and finisher of our faith. Be still and believe, let Jesus be Lord over all you're going through, this is the finish line. No matter what place we finish here the gift is still eternal life and there's nothing that can separate us from this love, for God's mercy is greater than His judgement.

Living in the third dimensional eternal my senses having 3D vision, and sense the spirit of God. It is in control of my body as I have yielded to His will over my own. I'm an open tomb resurrected from the 1st to the 3rd dimension. Jesus knows the way to the Father and His direction, for He always does the father's will and not His own. In one dimensional life, living in the flesh becomes a standard of self-gratification, as it seeks after its own to worship the creature rather than the creator. The god of self, to please the self will, over God's will just as the devil does. The devil is restricted to one dimension eating the dust as he's flast on His belly. When we focus on the Lord above, a vortex is created which raises us from the first to the third dimension. It is only in God's dimension we're able to contain life, as 3-D cups we can be filled, unlike that of the flat dimension. The devil's hold on us is broken, our minds are kept in perfect peace when stayed on the subject of the object of the eternal, Jesus Christ. As long as we don't return to timebase vision and break fellowship with God we're free. The devil will try and lure us back with deception, but don't give in to misperceptions, stay true to the voice of God and He will lead you. John 12:27 Now is my soul troubled and what shall I say? Father, "Save me from this hour: but for this cause came I unto this hour." Busy by faith not by our efforts we are saved from the flat dimension. Without God's word we are spinning around in the dark and have no light for direction. Watch and pray for the spirit is willing but the flesh is weak. We're the children of God, the world does not know us, but remember we know each other as His light is in us.

Lord give me strength as I yield to your direction vs. I have everything under control. Unraveling these two voices is the great conflict of life and death. For these are the DNA of orderly vs. disorderly conduct. I see God's will goes before birth. When we are offered a so-called blessing we can't receive it, when we're focused on the voice of a past dimensional influence; rather than on the voice of the King of heaven and the desire to receive His blessing for life. When I read of your word, answer your word in conversation, as I talk in my mind or aloud, I establish a relationship with God and know I am blessed for His love is always here with us. When self claims to have all the answers its scope becomes flat due to the limits of its predeterminations. Having all the answers to keep 'self' comfortable it does not venture out any further than it has to. Self is contained in its own orbit, me at the center, unless a catastrophe upsets the balance exposing the lie of its existence of disorder. It will be doomed never to experience the full spectrum of life, as the self can only see what it can know in time, not what being bonded to God can see, where I am and where the blessings are flowing from, the eternal. God wants to bless us with His dimension. Only the voice of the devil has most of us convinced there's only a single dimension, and to gravitate back to it. No matter how many times or ways God tries to get our attention. John 3.1 Behold what manner of love the father has given unto us that we should be called the children of God! Therefore the world does not know us, because it did not know Him. Three dimensional believers can acknowledge each other for they can see what is not true when held up to the line of God's order who is Jesus Christ. First, they see the condition of the other people. Second, they can put themselves in place of others and experience genuine compassion. Third, know when love and truth line up for life. Fourth, respond with wisdom discerning the situation at hand, and fifth, are able to speak when God opens their mouth as they recognize the fellowship of the Holy Spirit. They'll also see the enlarged spectrum plains of each other's spaces; whereas a one dimensional space will attempt, unknowingly, to bring one back from the third dimension by denying their eternal life reality, by trying to cause them to focus on the sin man nature. Getting a believer to endorse sin causes them to break fellowship with God. Once this is realized and the believer repents, this causes them access to do the will of the Father by following Jesus once again. When all the deviations to do the Father's will are removed, three dimensional eternal life is restored, as is oneness to the Father till the next growth pain taps us on the shoulder and points the way to God calling, "You can do it, take that first step, I'll catch you if you fall." John 8:51, B. "If a man keeps my saying he shall never see death." As when spaces get filled in to become solid with the truth of God.

No more walking between the dots as they've become connected as sharing unity. Now I move with them and it is life. I'm a new creation in Christ Jesus. John 4: 9, 10. In this the love of God was manifested towards us, that God sent His only begotten son into the world that we might live through Him. Not that we loved Him first, but God loved us and sent Jesus for the propitiation for our sins to be apart of His body as a believer, joined forever by the bond of love and His peace. In the face of all trials we're to belong to God. We prove this way by calling on God and not our own devicefullness of our ways which please the self. Stand therefore when temptation comes being faithful to call upon the Lord, to turn the heat to light and deposit treasures in heaven, enlarging your space at the same time answering the mark of the highest calling to be true to where love comes from, the cross. Men seek God their own way, but only those who cry out for help are brought in by the spirit of God. Don't get mad at people, get mad at the devil which blinds their minds; then invite them in to come and dine. Christ in us! Can we identify with this for handling our affairs (in our space), we grow free as we rest to do the father's will in Him. Identifying with God's word = Christ sanctified = us (the body), by grace as free. Rev. 3:20. Behold I stand at the door and knock. If anyone hears my voice and opens the door, I will come in to him and dine with him, and he with me.

There's an entering in to God's country, as we seek Him we enter into His will. As ambassadors for Christ, we're Christians living in another world, but dwell in embassies of God's dominion. We are a refuge in a world of famine for others to enter in. People who don't know God are looking for answers, they see people and goals as mountains. They try to climb them to see what's at the top to know if it's what they want too. As we maintain an attitude of prayer we become mountains for others and mountain climbers on God's mountain. Only we know as we're lifted from the flat plain of time into third dimensional eternal life, what God has to offer us by His word, a splendid awesome majestic heaven. We know where we are going. Look up ahead, don't lose your footing. Having become semi-familiar with God's turane, I look back and see how far I've come and raising the banners of past victories I become more thankful as I continue to climb. I gain height into the eternal where God sustains me with His life. Something is always renewed to become new on my journey as I pray. Along my way I keep sight of the light for my life as I know Jesus who climbed before me, to show me the way. I'm in 3D love and it's grand for this kind of love gets me through dead flat everyday days alive, knowing my Savior is holding my hand. Know that we are of God, and the whole world lies under the sway of the wicked one. Knowing the son of God has given us understanding that we may know who is true; and we are in Him who is true, in His son Jesus Christ. This is the true God and Eternal Life.

Lord help me, change me, to remain vulnerable that I may be real. I need to be sensitive to your touch, that your love may flow to me and through me, to bring healing to a hurting world. We're connected to each other in the body and are not alone. I embrace you Lord Jesus my King; you are my final word and first love. I'm convinced You will make disciples of all who call on You for life, as I've grown in You through knowledge and grace, I've come to know putting You first Lord Jesus everything else will fall into place. I've become insufficient, that Christ may be my sufficiency in all, amen.

15

Diagrams

By the grace of God, which I thank Him for, this book was finished in His timing. God You do not work according to our plans. I've learned the highest place on earth is at the foot of Your cross and to wait prayerfully patiently upon You daily, (always room for improvement), there's life here. Lord Jesus, you shed your own blood to cleanse us from our sins and by grace I trust you will complete your work in us. We're to rest in this trust and experience your peace within and worship you Jesus with a conscience contact of your reality, (faith).

I've included some diagrams to help us to better understand, the new birth of the eternal, the reality of Christ through grace as a spontaneous act of love, keeping my eyes on Jesus Christ in us, to will, and to do His good pleasure is life, also by His grace. Life is a task which prepares us for growth. As we journey on we go forward in the name of Jesus, we know that He'll be there to preserve His honor. Traveling on the right path we are in the light just as He is in the light.

When I lose sight of Jesus I get comfortable in my old ways, just long enough to remember there's no life in them. I then remember the Master and my heart soars with joy, freedom from the doldrums of death. I have left I am set free. Eternal life has expanded me even more than the reality of time itself giving me the reinforcement I need to continue to stand in my new identity. I've become a child of Jesus Christ. I'm alive and my senses thrill to His touch. When annoyed the more I realize there's still yet more I've to turn over to God. Sudden surprise pressures spring up, still tendencies to want to take control without consulting God first. I can see, this suggests to me how far I've grown. I'm so grateful God is patient with me. Even though He was tempted in all things, He waits for me with compassion and loves me through the very trials He Himself endured. Jesus never shouts, "Get in line!" He just stands beside me and holds my hand. I'm left in awe, He knows my heart, mind, my soul

125

and speaks to me even though I may not listen. Then I'll mess up and stop and stand, hear, to the move of His voice. I've strayed from His land. Surrender to His word I must, as it is life. No longer to wander, for now I know when I'm in control God is not. So I surrender all for now, till next I stray. I'll always find to grow again is me and you. For this is what we do, as we're renewed. The Bible events are happening right now and as we read them we enter in crossing over to eternity from time, this is life, the walls of time are falling down. We overcome it by the blood of Jesus and by the word of our testimony; and that we love not our own lives unto death only excepting the eternal. I can see the road ahead as one to where I'm going to. God's country entering in, all the way in. It is Jesus I see, to escape the oblivion of Hell. He turns our evil eye from the heart; into His guiding eye that will rejoice forevermore. Love is a seed of light planted in a dark world.

We touch Jesus through His word and become apart of His body when we believe. How many of us consider our minds as they gather up thoughts throughout the day continually. Do we ever question, turn to the source from which they come from and know it. These diagrams explore our reasoning. In review keep in mind that 'Truth Constant' is the Bible.

Maximum Perception

Balance

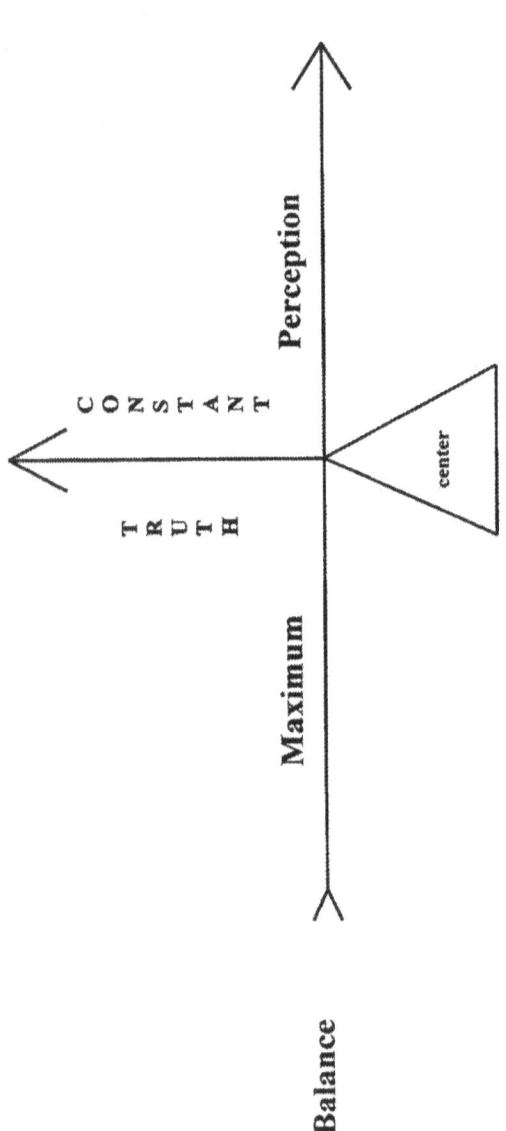

When our center is in line with truth constant we have our balance and maximum perception for growth.

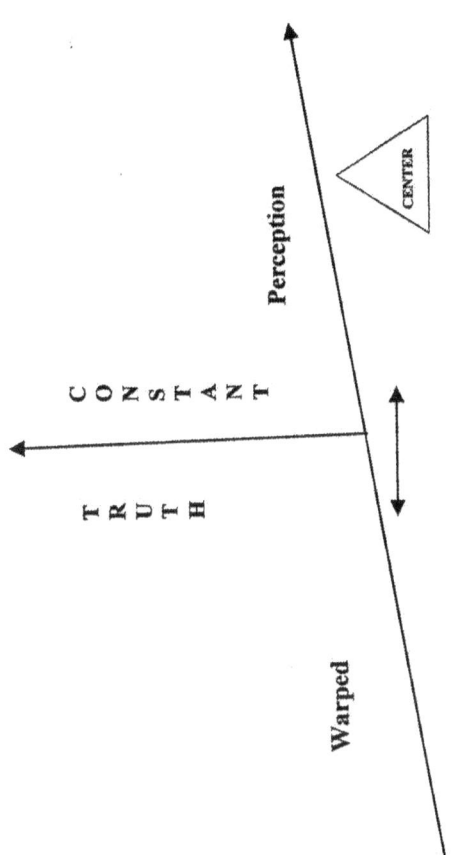

Perception

CONSTANT

TRUTH

Warped

CENTER

Without 'truth constant' in line, a center will continually shift due to a lack of direction. This causes warped or misperception on how we're to grow for the balance will always be off.

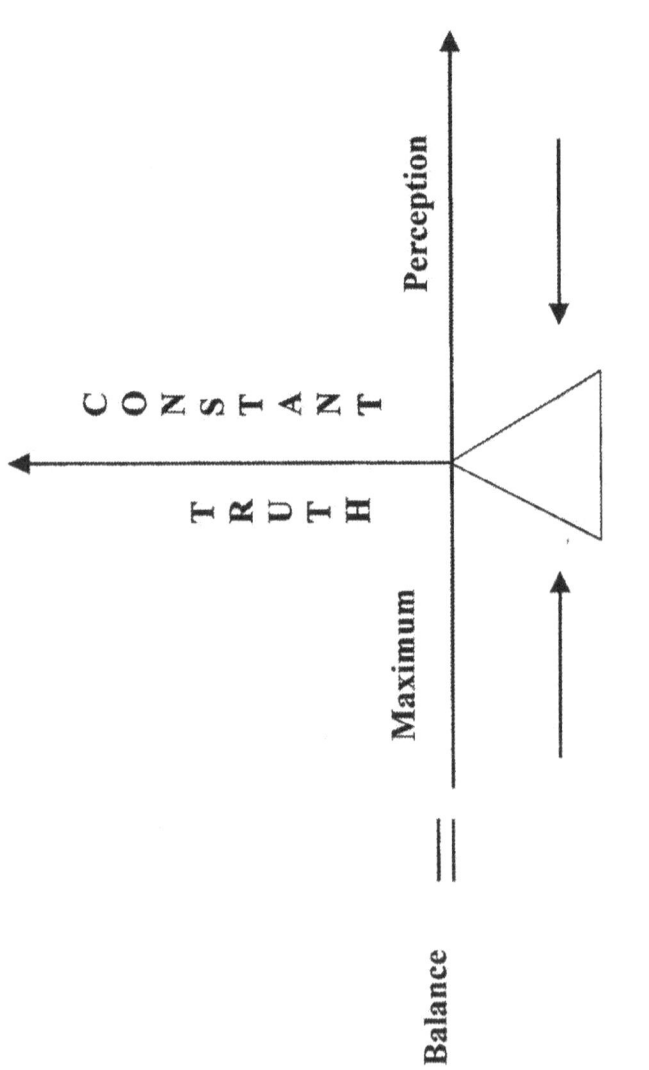

It is only when a center lines up with 'truth constant' eternal growth takes place and our lives become enlarged.

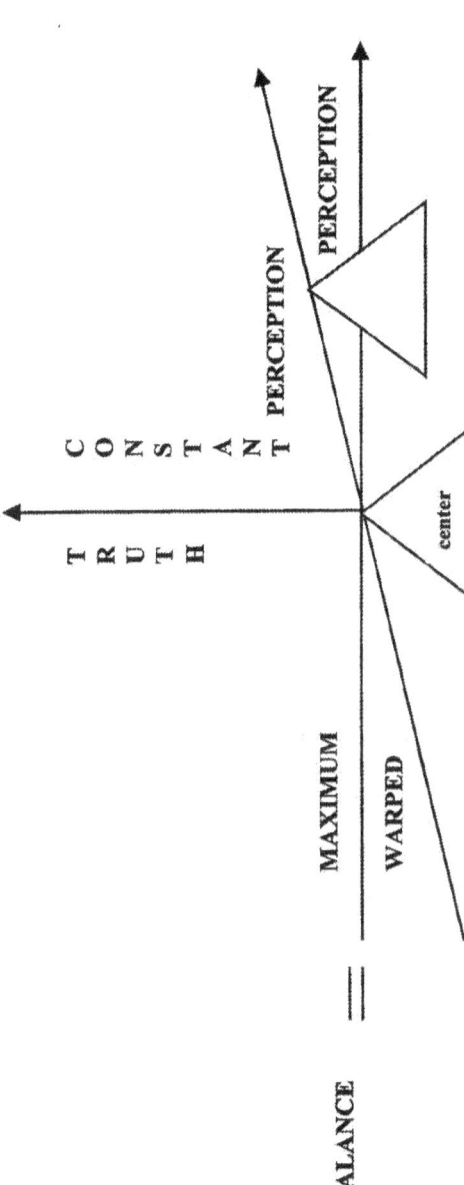

Balance is built over a period of time. We learn what is eternal for life as balance, 'truth constant', and our centers, (comprised of thoughts and emotions), all line up. Learning the difference between what has order and what is false, out of order, trains all of our senses towards what is our focus for eternal life.

Limitations === NO Growth

Truth
Non-existent

Limitations

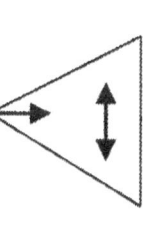

Base without focal point.

Without a focal point to start from our limitations keep us from growth, due to non-consistent truth. There's no vision to sustain life. No balance for direction.

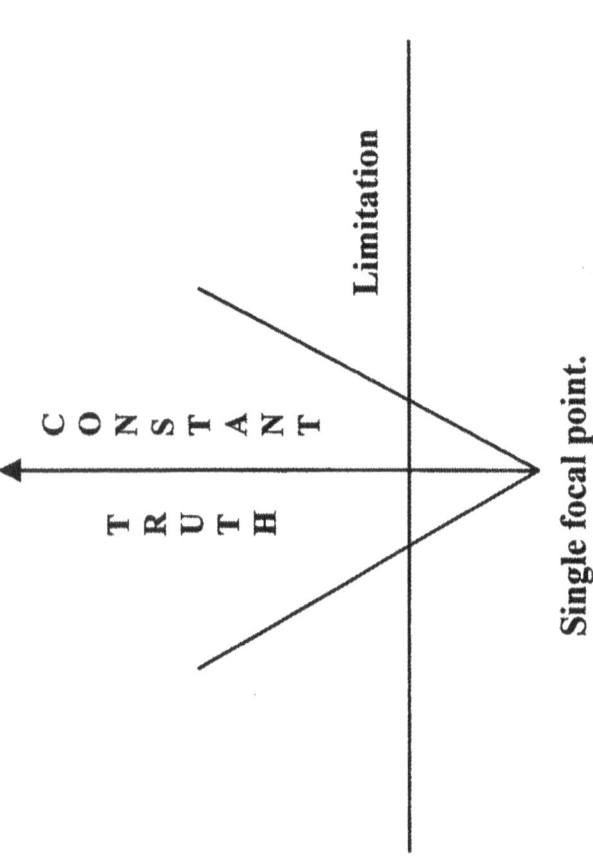

CONSTANT TRUTH

Limitation

Single focal point.

When our focus is single we are able to build on what is 'Truth Constant' and grow, exceeding our limitations for maximum life potential. We have balance and direction.

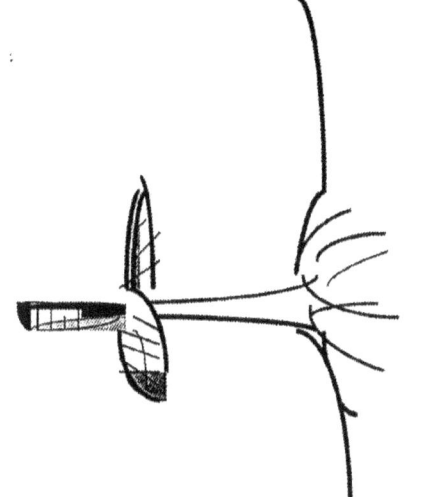

Can man produce an original seed to produce life from the darkness of the soil beneath the earth? There is a given truth to every seed.

When our focus is single on a 'truth constant' seed, a structure will arise with an order that will promote growth. Enlarging to sustain more life and overcome our limitations.

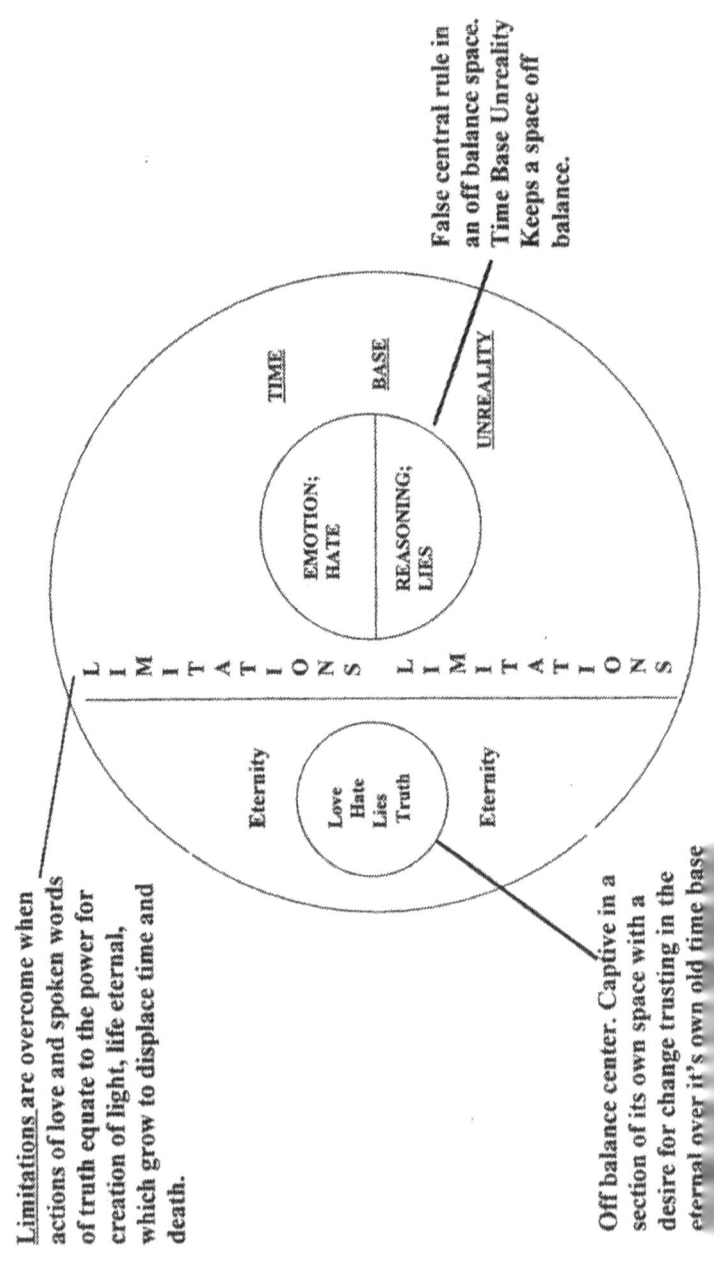

False central rule in an off balance space. Time Base Unreality Keeps a space off balance.

Limitations are overcome when actions of love and spoken words of truth equate to the power for creation of light, life eternal, which grow to displace time and death.

Off balance center. Captive in a section of its own space with a desire for change trusting in the eternal over it's own old time base

TIME

BASE

UNREALITY

EMOTION; HATE

REASONING; LIES

L I M I T A T I O N S

L I M I T A T I O N S

Eternity

Eternity

Love
Hate
Lies
Truth

136

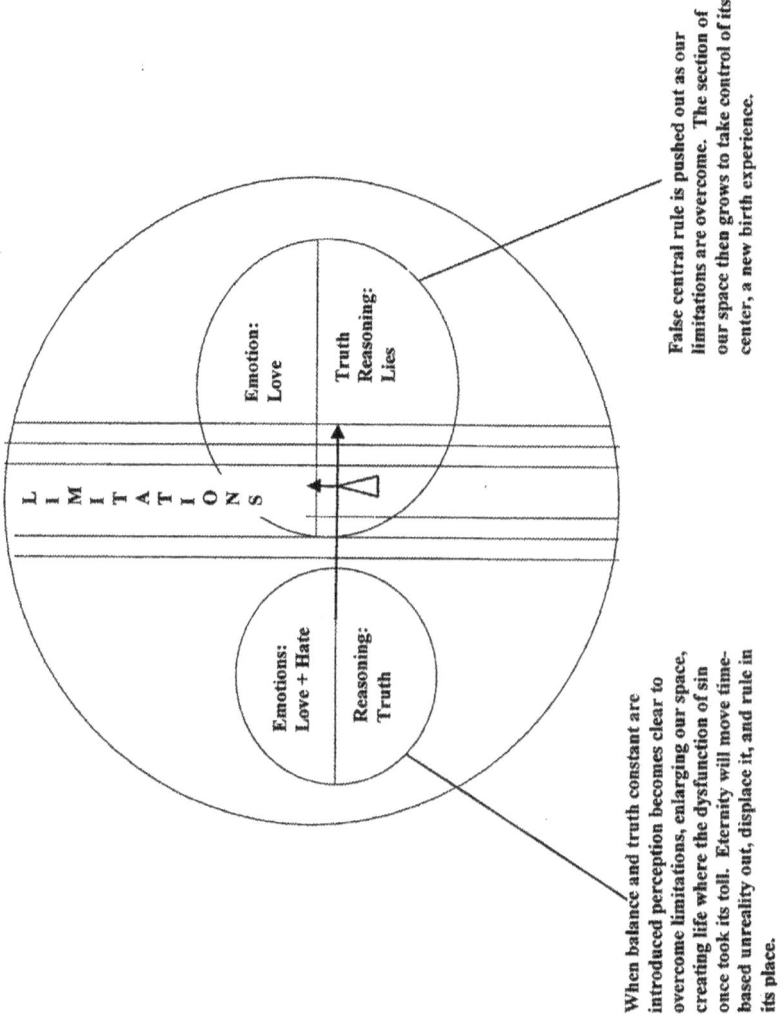

When balance and truth constant are introduced perception becomes clear to overcome limitations, enlarging our space, creating life where the dysfunction of sin once took its toll. Eternity will move time-based unreality out, displace it, and rule in its place.

False central rule is pushed out as our limitations are overcome. The section of our space then grows to take control of its center, a new birth experience.

Emotion: Love
Truth
Reasoning: Lies

Emotions: Love + Hate
Reasoning: Truth

L
I
M
I
T
A
T
I
O
N
S

137

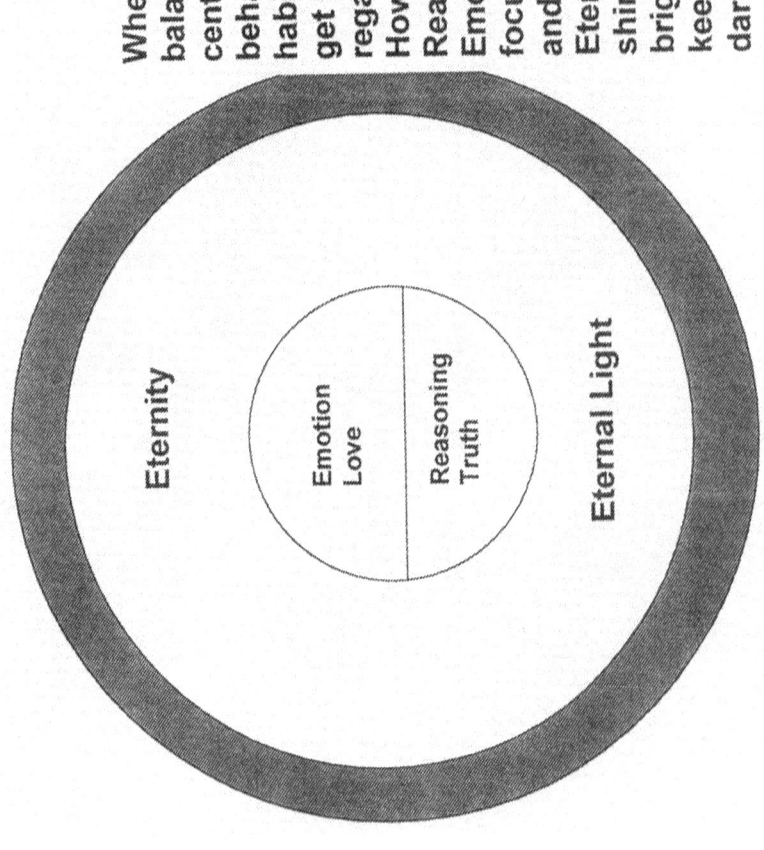

When there's balance within a center, old behavioral sin habits fight to get back in to regain control. However, when Reasoning and Emotions are focused on Love and Truth the Eternal Light shines so brightly Jesus keeps all darkness out.

Eternity

Emotion
Love

Reasoning
Truth

Eternal Light

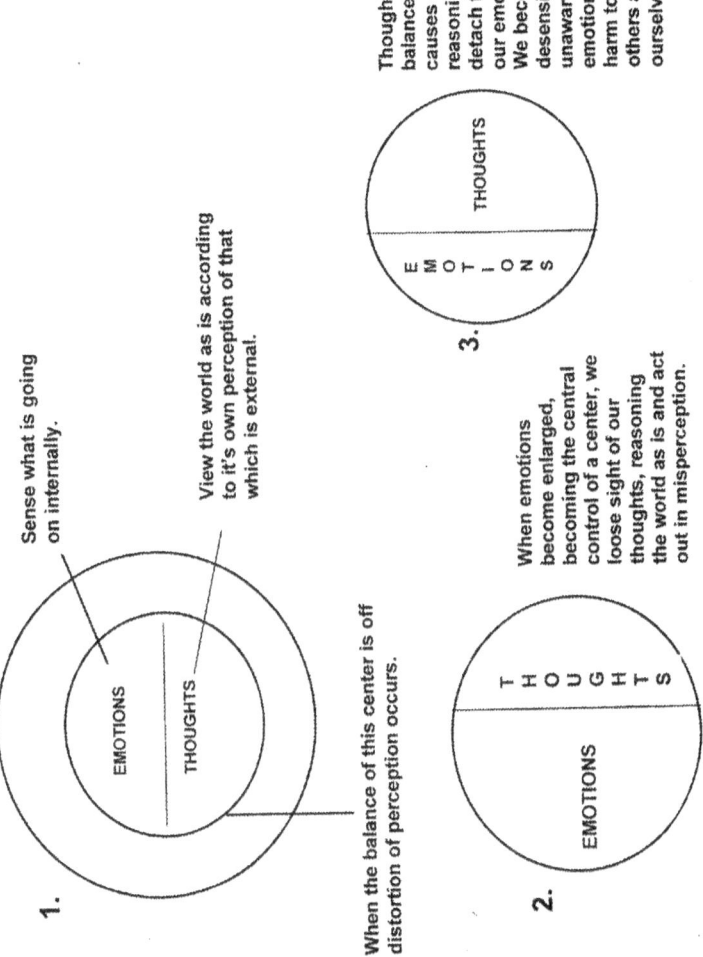

1.

Sense what is going on internally.

View the world as is according to it's own perception of that which is external.

EMOTIONS

THOUGHTS

When the balance of this center is off distortion of perception occurs.

2.

THOUGHTS

EMOTIONS

When emotions become enlarged, becoming the central control of a center, we loose sight of our thoughts, reasoning the world as is and act out in misperception.

3.

EMOTIONS

THOUGHTS

Thoughts off balance causes our reasoning to detach from our emotions. We become desensitized, unaware of emotional harm to others and ourselves.

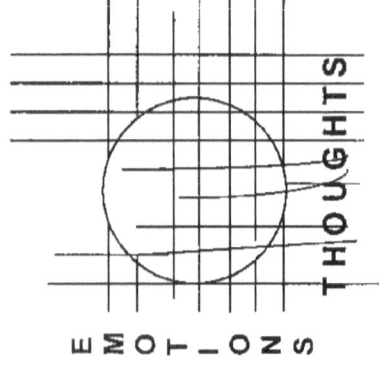

THOUGHTS

EMOTIONS

When a feeling
grid is in order
there is rest, all
thoughts and
emotions are in
sync. The mind
has peace, vision
is clear to the
eternal.

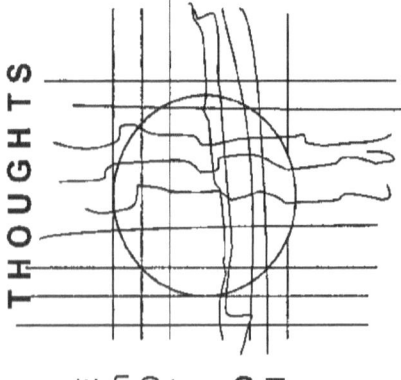

THOUGHTS

EMOTIONS

When stress is
present do to
conflict too fast to
process
depression occurs,
vision gets
distorted, it
becomes limited to
time.

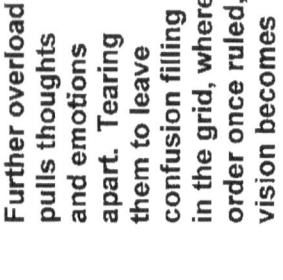

THOUGHTS

EMOTIONS

Further overload
pulls thoughts
and emotions
apart. Tearing
them to leave
confusion filling
in the grid, where
order once ruled,
vision becomes
further distorted.

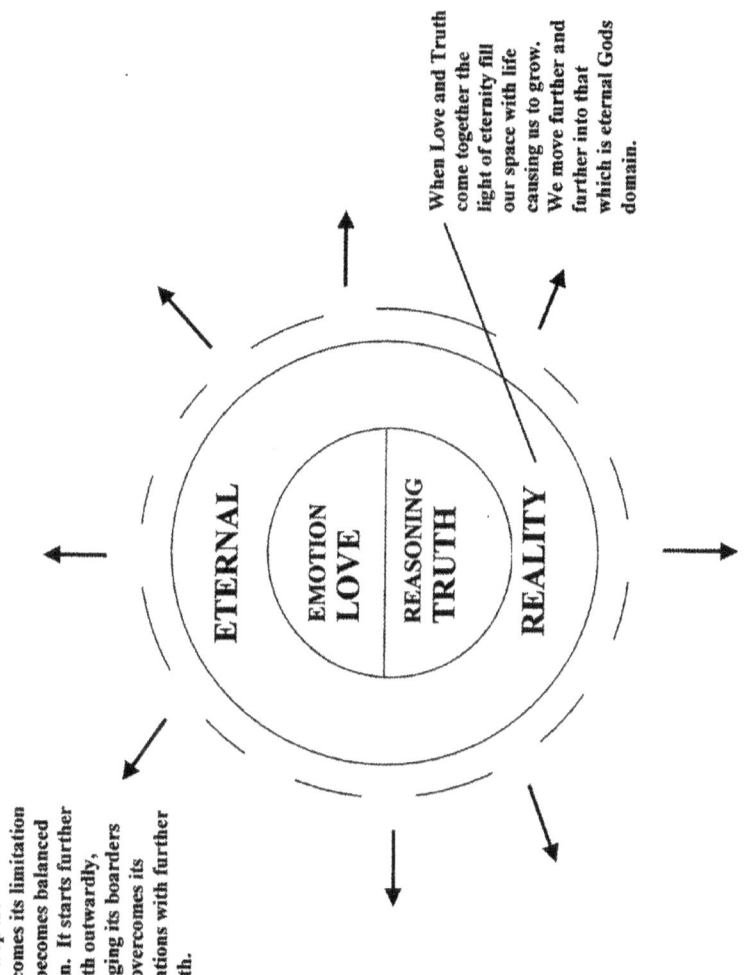

When Love and Truth come together the light of eternity fill our space with life causing us to grow. We move further and further into that which is eternal Gods domain.

ETERNAL

EMOTION
LOVE

REASONING
TRUTH

REALITY

After a space overcomes its limitation and becomes balanced within. It starts further growth outwardly, enlarging its boarders as it overcomes its limitations with further growth.

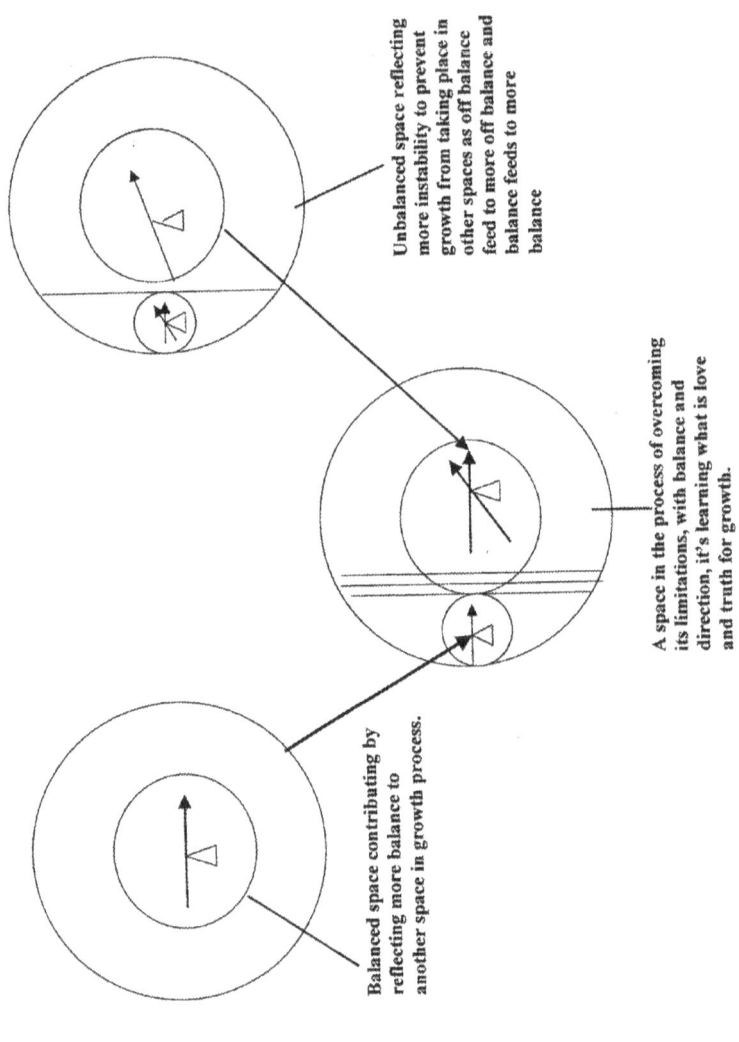

Unbalanced space reflecting more instability to prevent growth from taking place in other spaces as off balance feed to more off balance and balance feeds to more balance

A space in the process of overcoming its limitations, with balance and direction, it's learning what is love and truth for growth.

Balanced space contributing by reflecting more balance to another space in growth process.

142

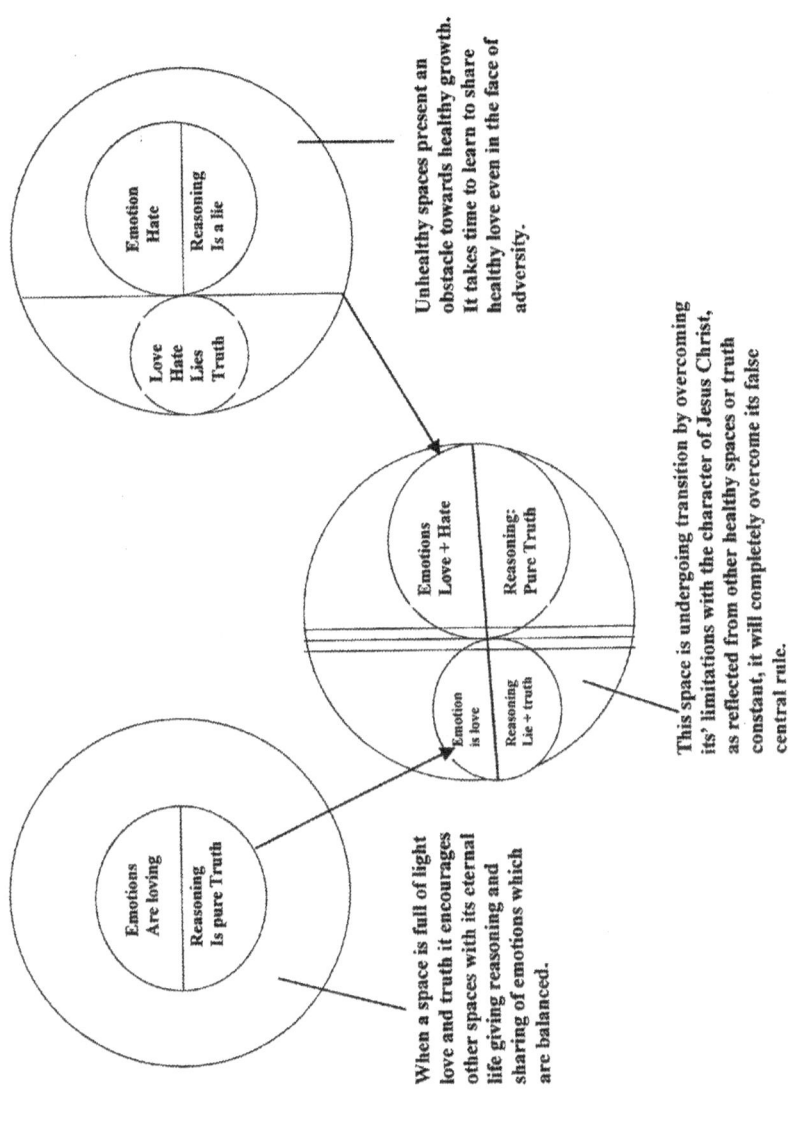

Unhealthy spaces present an obstacle towards healthy growth. It takes time to learn to share healthy love even in the face of adversity.

Emotion Hate | Reasoning Is a lie

Love
Hate
Lies
Truth

This space is undergoing transition by overcoming its' limitations with the character of Jesus Christ, as reflected from other healthy spaces or truth constant, it will completely overcome its false central rule.

Emotions Love + Hate | Reasoning: Pure Truth

Emotion is love | Reasoning Lie + truth

When a space is full of light love and truth it encourages other spaces with its eternal life giving reasoning and sharing of emotions which are balanced.

Emotions Are loving | Reasoning Is pure Truth

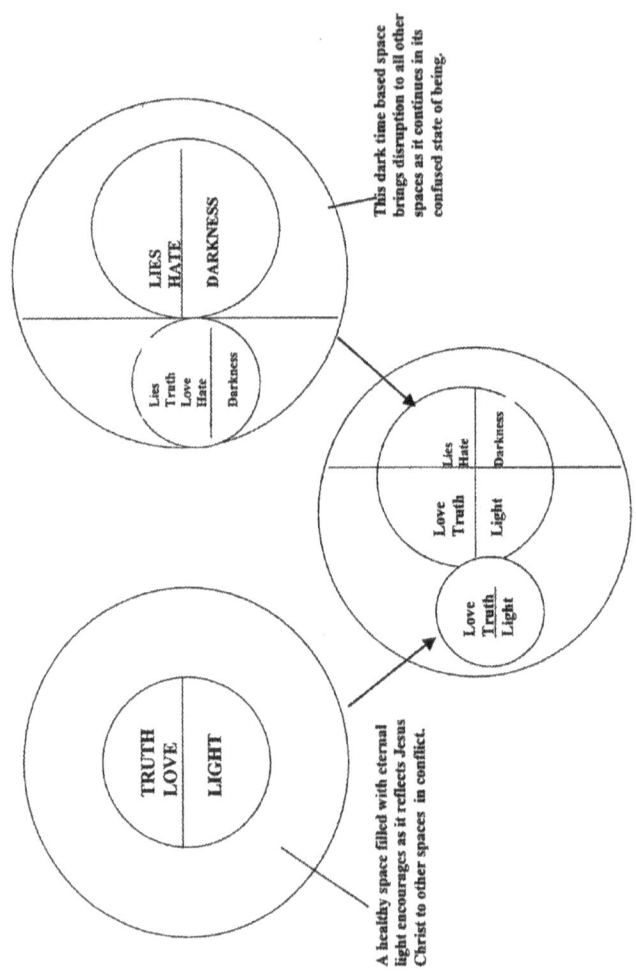

This dark time based space brings disruption to all other spaces in its confused state of being.

LIES
HATE
DARKNESS

Lies
Truth
Love
Hate
Darkness

Lies
Hate
Darkness

Love Truth
Light

Love
Truth
Light

TRUTH
LOVE
LIGHT

A healthy space filled with eternal light encourages as it reflects Jesus Christ to other spaces in conflict.

This space has grown to a position where its false center has become the smaller section and with its new eternal center its prospects are good for replacing its darkness with the light of Jesus Christ.

Perceptual Balance

LOVE

Love + Truth = Light

Reality, Eternal
In Order

Unreality, time based
Out of Order

TRUTH

LIES
+ HATE
= DARKNESS

Perceptual Balance

LOVE + Truth = Light

LOVE

Reality, Eternal In Order

Unreality, Time based Out of Order

TRUTH

LIES + THE DARKNESS

Transformation Zone: A space stands against darkness for the love of truth till darkness is finally burned away and light takes its place.

1. When at the end of reason, all we comprehend is nothing; we then face instability with all the uncertainties.

2. Falling over the edge of reason we realize there's a need for order, seeing there's no structure we cry-out for help. If God is missed transformation does not take place; the space becomes lost continually and searches for further understanding on another plain of unreality.

3. Without structure there is no control, minus control no balance, and insanity starts to set in as we fall from unreality, with oblivion and darkness staring us in the face instead of the structure of God's light.

4. Jesus breaks this cycle by bringing eternal reality to this structure, and stability in place of instability. Transformation then starts to take place.

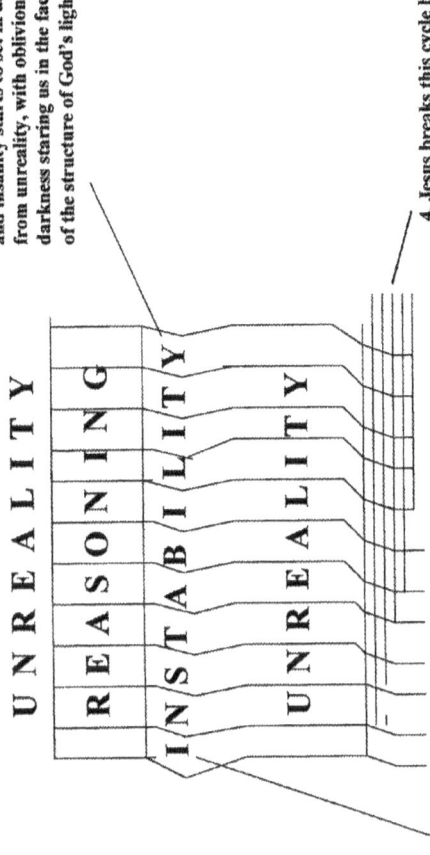

UNREALITY

REASONING

INSTABILITY

UNREALITY

Perceptual Balance

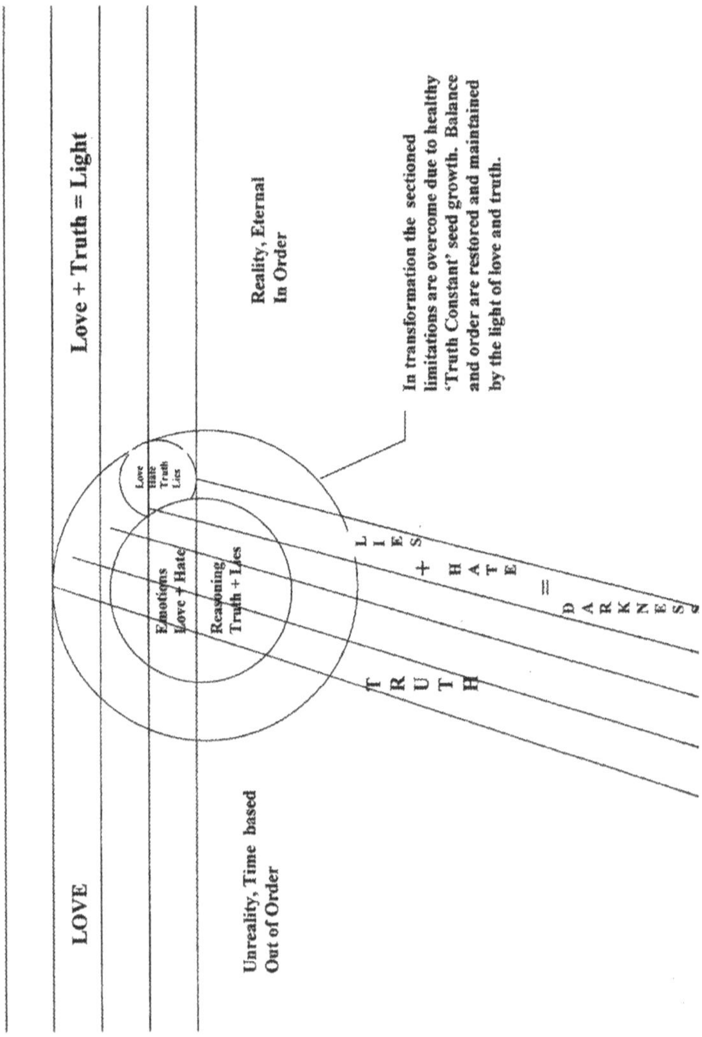

LOVE

Love + Truth = Light

Unreality, Time based
Out of Order

Reality, Eternal
In Order

Love
Hate
Truth
Lies

Emotions
Love + Hate

Reasoning
Truth + Lies

T
R
U
T
H

L
I
E
S
+
H
A
T
E
=
D
A
R
K
N
E
S
S

In transformation the sectioned
limitations are overcome due to healthy
'Truth Constant' seed growth. Balance
and order are restored and maintained
by the light of love and truth.

148

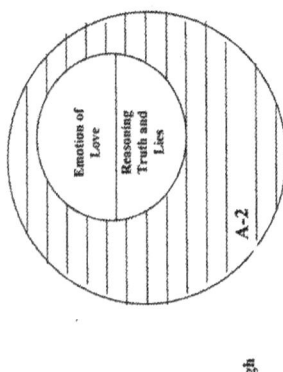

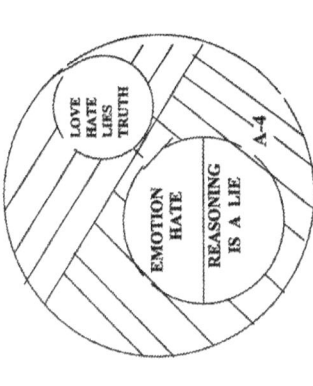

A-1: When we have eternal balance our center rests in the middle of our space, after a successful transformation.

A-2: When we exceed the limitations of our growth rate, try to obtain something we're not ready for, then our center shifts in our space towards its outer limits. If it does not return to order by re-establishing conscience contact with Eternal Reality, then a lie(darkness), is open to come in because the space is hurting itself through self hatred.

A-3: The center of the space goes into denial and looses its healthy Love + Truth = Light perception.

A-4: The person takes on a false identity and becomes sectioned off, (a prisoner), in its own space; as Darkness = lies + hate have taken over control of its center.

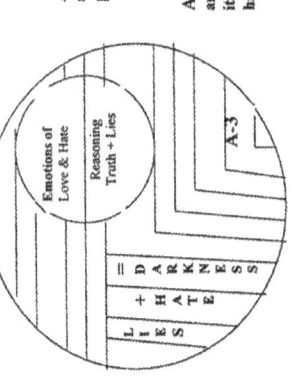

149

LIGHT

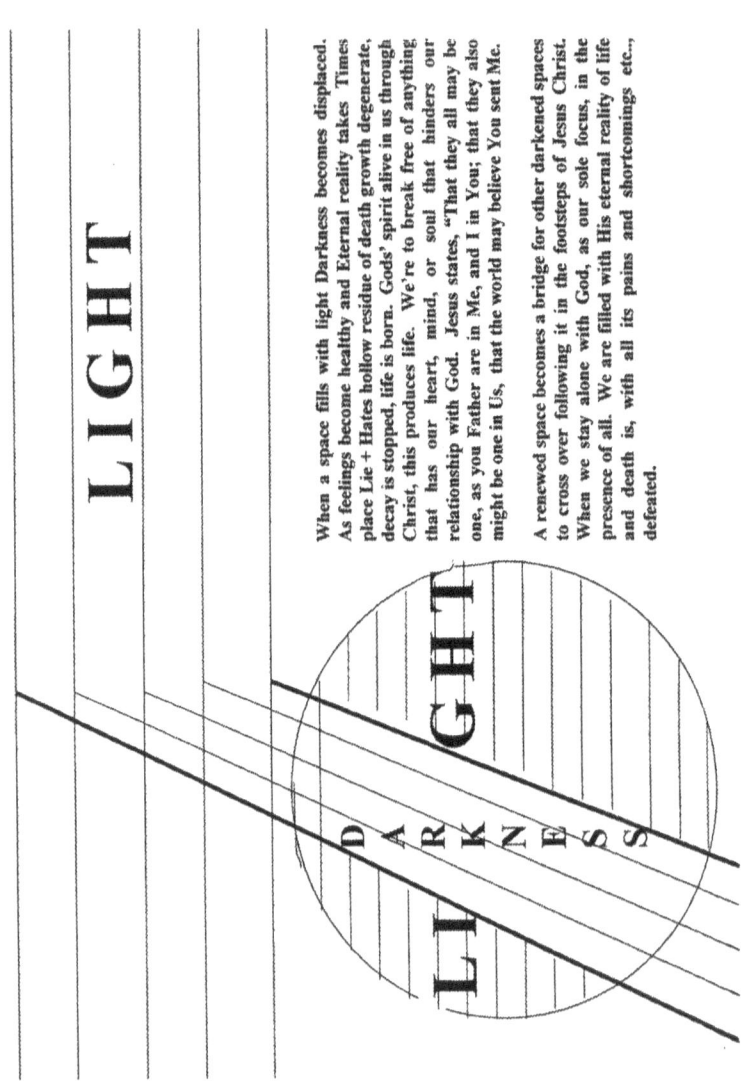

When a space fills with light Darkness becomes displaced. As feelings become healthy and Eternal reality takes Times place Lie + Hates hollow residue of death growth degenerate, decay is stopped, life is born. Gods' spirit alive in us through Christ, this produces life. We're to break free of anything that has our heart, mind, or soul that hinders our relationship with God. Jesus states, "That they all may be one, as you Father are in Me, and I in You; that they also might be one in Us, that the world may believe You sent Me.

A renewed space becomes a bridge for other darkened spaces to cross over following it in the footsteps of Jesus Christ. When we stay alone with God, as our sole focus, in the presence of all. We are filled with His eternal reality of life and death is, with all its pains and shortcomings etc.., defeated.

DARKNESS

LIGHT

Fig, A- The spirit of the Living God giving off eternal light.

Fig. B- A spiritually dark flow separated from God, with a dark space.

Fig. C- When we go against the dark flow and start to reflect Gods light, by standing still to experience Gods life, it causes friction which generates heat which burns away the darkness adding more light.

Fig. D- When a space comes to rest in the Eternal flame light increases one line at a time until the space is completely set free from the dark flow, filled with light, and fully connected to eternity.

Fig. E- Although the dark flow tries as space E. continues to walk with God daily, the darkness remains locked out and the space is set free.

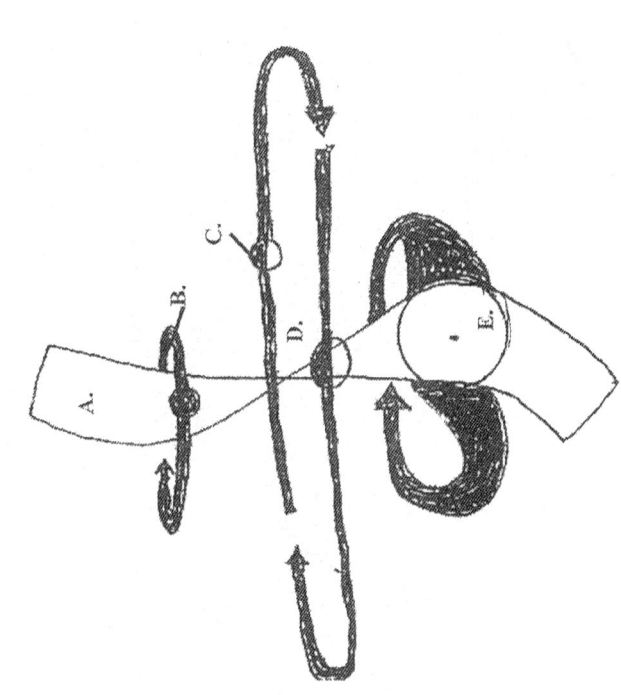

Fig. A – The spirit and eternal flame of God full of life. The center of order holding all life in position, the axle of the hub.

Fig. B- Everyone who gravitates to the spokes unites with Gods out reaching Love and truth to connect with His light, and bonds with His order.

Fig. C- The rim is full of darkness, a place without life except for where the spokes make conscience contact with seeking spaces, hungr for the life giving spirit of God,

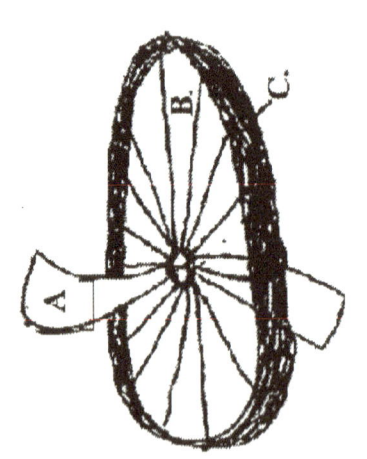

Eternity is balanced as is truth.

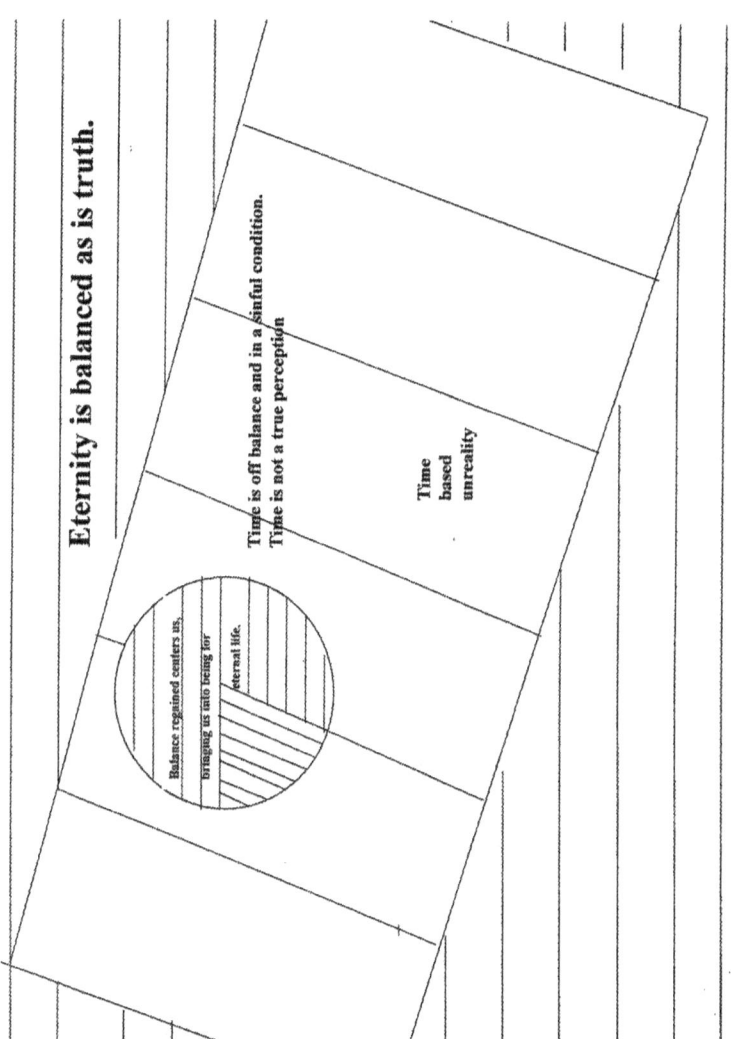

Time is off balance and in a sinful condition.
Time is not a true perception

Time
based
unreality

Balance regained centers us,

bringing us into being for

eternal life.

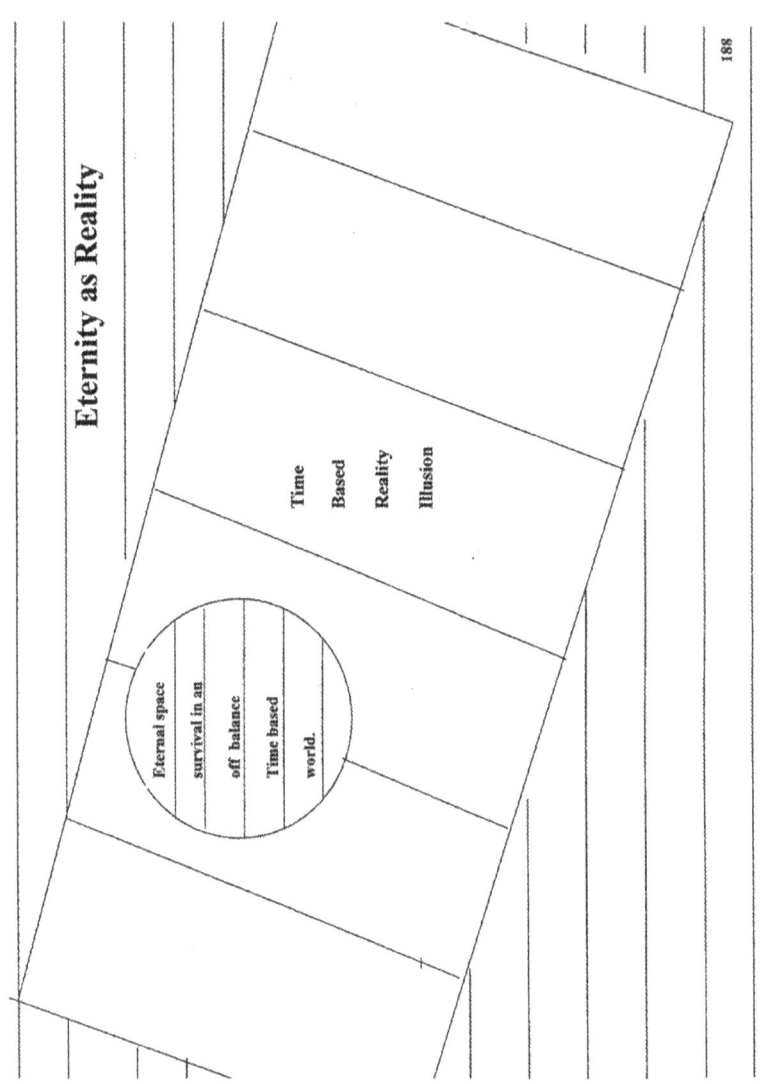

Eternity as Reality

Time
Based
Reality
Illusion

Eternal space
survival in an
off balance
Time based
world.

Perceptual Balance

Eternity has Eternal Reality

Love + Truth = Light

Action + Spoken Word

Emotion: Love | Reasoning: Truth

= Power for Creation

When Action, our Emotions and Spoken Word, our Reasoning are Love + Truth, Power for Creation will yield light revealing Jesus Christ the way to go for life eternal.

LOVE

TRUTH

TIME

BASED UNREALITY

HATE + LIES = DARKNESS

189

155

Perceptual Balance

Eternity

Eternal Reality

Love + Truth = Light

LOVE

Action + Spoken Word

Emotions; Love | Reasoning: Lies + Truth

= Power for Creation

TRUTH

TIME

BASED UNREALITY = DARKNESS

HATE + LIES = DARKNESS

When Action and spoken word stem from unbalanced emotions and reasoning, power for creation yields darkness in a time base unreality keeping us from the light of life, Jesus Christ.

Perceptual Balance

Eternity

Eternal Reality

Love + Truth = Light

Action + Spoken Word

Competition for Central

= Power for Creation

LOVE

TRUTH

TIME

THAT ELIMINATES DARKNESS

TIME

These spiritual flows effect our everyday lives. Eternity enlarges our space while time keeps us limited in its own flow. Our actions and spoken words that we choose yield power for creation, darkness always try's to keep our senses dark sighted as light tries to show us the way to eternal life. Our choices build us towards life or death as these spiritual forces compete for our soul, life being when visible.

157

Perceptual Balance

Eternity

Eternal Reality

Love + Truth = Light

LOVE

T
R
U
T
H

T
I
M
E

B
A
S
E
D

M
E

H
A
T
E
+
L
I
E
S
=
D
A
R
K
N
E
S
S

What God Sees As Best

JESUS

For My Life

Power for
creation yields
death or life

God is sufficient bringing contentment,
Christ centered and eternal satisfaction.
Eternal spectrum reveals to us the nature of
our condition and gives direction for change,
as we call upon God for completion, change
occurs.

What I want to

ME

Make Me Happy

Discontentment keeps us
searching for time
gratification of self-fulfillment.
We're limited without eternal
truth to show us the whole
spectrum of life.

158

Perceptual Balance

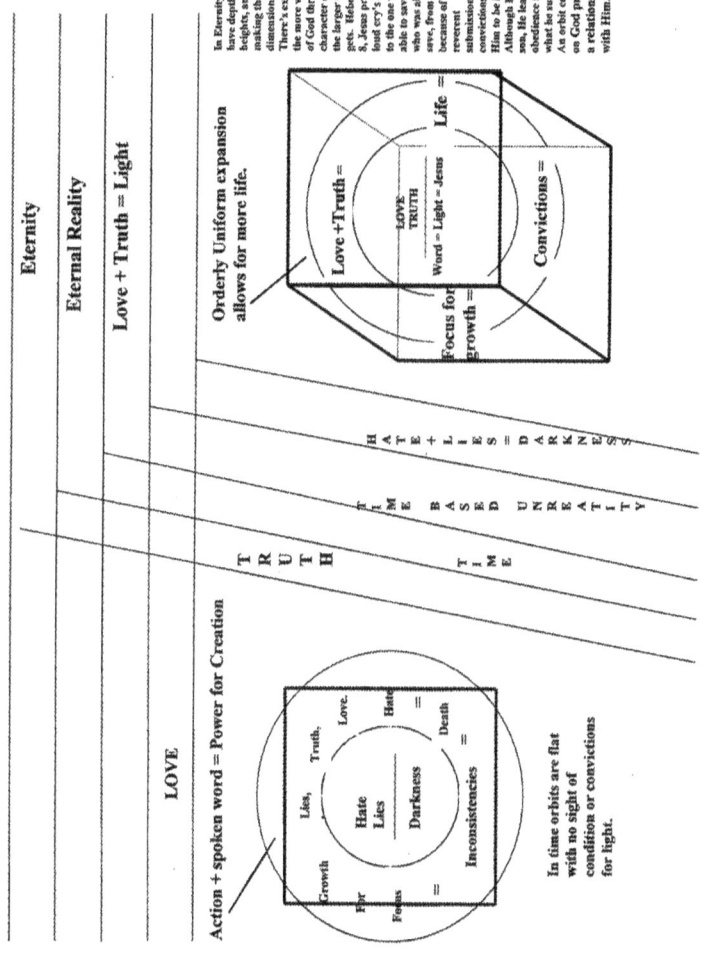

Eternity

Eternal Reality

Love + Truth = Light

Orderly Uniform expansion allows for more life.

Love + Truth =

Life =

Focus for growth

Convictions =

LOVE
TRUTH
Word = Light = Jesus

In Eternity orbits have depths, widths, heights, and breadths making them three-dimensional.

There's expansion, the more we learn of God through the character of Jesus, the larger the cube gets. Hebrews 5:7-8, Jesus prayed with loud cry's and tears to the one who was able to save Him, who was able to save, from death because of His reverent submission, (His convictions), caused Him to be heard. Although He was a son, He learned obedience from what he suffered. As orbit centered on God promotes a relationship with Him.

TRUTH

HATE + LIES = DARKNESS

TIME

FOR ME BASED

TIME

LOVE

Action + spoken word = Power for Creation

Lies, Truth, Love. Hate

Growth

For Focus

Hate Lies Darkness

Death =

Inconsistencies =

In time orbits are flat with no sight of condition or convictions for light.

159

Perceptual Balance

Eternity

Eternal Reality

Love + Truth = Light

As growth takes place the space is lifted from the flat dimension of Time to the third dimension of Eternity.

Unlimited full spectrum of Eternal Reality dimension.

LOVE

Action

+

Love
Truth

Spoken
Word

Hate
Lies

Darkness

Light

=

Creation

for

Power

Transformation occurs when we look towards eternity with Power for creation, our space begins to expand with three dimensional life. We start to grow out from having a self center to taking on a Christ center.

HATE + LIES = DARKNESS

BASED UNREATHINESS

TIME

TRUTH

Limited flat dimension spectrum of Time.

160

-16-
Insights

These insights are not to add, but to build on who's already there, Jesus Christ. Reading the Bible advances us into and through His light.

1. Jesus needs to be more real than the air we breath.
2. When we realize we're naked then God can clothe us.
3. It's not always our words but God's timing in which we use them that make a difference.
4. Jesus was alone with God when He walked among men on the earth.
5. I'm learning of the Joy of grace and how to be still in the freedom of it.
6. There's nowhere else to go for life but God.
7. When words are spoken in haste they take us where we do not want to go.
8. God's Spirit alone produced life in us.
9. Light is a door to another world in the midst of darkness.
10. People choose little things to try to satisfy big needs.
11. The things of Time can never satisfy Eternal needs.
12. Who we surrender to is who we'll become.
13. A yielded vessel to God brings honor, life and health wherever it flows.
14. We become the music we listen to.
15. God indwells those who cry out and worship Him.
16. Life is an adventure. We never know who or what we'll meet on our way towards heaven, but know this: it'll help us to grow.
17. When we take light, the Eternal fire, for granted, there's a tendency to focus on the shadows of the particles which burn away from the light. Don't be enticed to dwell in darkness as a particle slave.
18. Things built upon insanity will never last, whereas those built upon God's word will last forever, God satisfies.

19. We show God worship by honoring His word.
20. Jesus sees us as we're joined to His word and the Holy Spirit shows us Jesus at all times.
21. To be complete in Christ is to be full of joy.
22. Are we to just survive, or to live by grace?
23. God wants to dwell with people who have room for Him in their lives.
24. What do we fill ourselves with all the day long? If it be praises to God, then all is well with my soul.
25. Whenever love and truth come together there's an atmosphere of light for us to see ourselves.
26. God's grace allows me to be me while I trust and walk, safely with Him, as I get introduced to change He changes me into new life.
27. Do we live with ourselves or with God? He can be, (without the world).
28. Confusion comes from knowing others without first considering God's character.
29. Don't try to fix life. Ask God for help and wait.
30. When I reflect over my past and all the mistakes I've made, I know there's still my future I have to face. As a speck in a cloud of dust, life is too big to handle. Got to trust God to lead me through and then to see my worth all the while.
31. Gravity exists whether it's believed or not. We must be in touch with what influences our lives or suffer fate instead of faith.
32. If we know not what to say we're to be patient and wait on God for direction. It's out of being with Christ good works will follow.
33. Still chewing and digesting, not ready for more, till I've fully taken in what I've just learned.
34. A river of living water is as to the Spirit of God. Whenever we call on Him He satisfies with the goodness of Jesus.
35. The word of God is to brick as prayer is to mortar. A house will not stand unless both are applied simultaneously.

36. When we recognize the character of Christ we're able to come out of ourselves to receive life from the eternal.
37. In order for a family to bond everyone must agree on the same source of love + truth = light for growth to expand the unit cohesively.
38. We've got to learn to speak by agreeing with love to remain alive.
39. Love is not something you feel. It is a language all of its own, that can make you feel better when you speak it.
40. Managing a healthy family is more important than that position of power, wealth, or prestige that the world has to offer. To honor God above all else has true lasting eternal value.
41. When we pray for others as our hearts become one with God, others are tugged in their hearts to come out of themselves and join God's reality in a deeper way.
42. There's no telling of the joy that will take the place of present discomforts as we honor God's will above our own, till all at last will be set in order, and our lives to be made whole.
43. When God's word goes forth eternity touches time and miracles flow.
44. If something does not glorify God flee from it.
45. We live in this world by the grace of God which brings us from disorder to order. God is always our friend.
46. One can see farthest from the top of the mountain. In the meantime we climb not to enjoy the view in the valley, but the glimpses as to what lay ahead.
47. Moved by the Spirit of God I dance, and then some more.
48. When we open the Bible we're in God's domain. To keep Eternity before us is life and health.
49. As knives get sharpened by stone so to those who live by the sword of the Spirit get sharper by stony hearts of those who oppose.
50. Love is a seed of light in a dark world, Jesus paid our way in full.

51. Can't force growth. Be patient, be true in the now. Let Christ work Christ in you.
52. It's a fight to be still when we hurt but we must to feel God's love, the presence of His touch.
53. Riding on the wings of the Spirit, life is a wonderful adventure. You never know what God's going to bring into light next on your journey.
54. In dealing with Children first be stern, then patient, and finally explain all your actions till they understand the situation thoroughly.
55. Be attentive, be watchful! Just when we think we know God, He reveals another aspect of Himself, and our view point becomes subject to change as we grow.
56. Seek compassion from God in prayer for He is generous.
57. Don't seek after material things. Let God give them to you as you grow obeying Him.
58. Do we see things as they are or the way we want to see them?
59. Hope is to believe God's word is God's word.
60. A gift gets bigger each time you share it.
61. We talk when we say nothing, silence sends a message.
62. It is God's grace that He will not let us out of His care.
63. When I stopped trying to figure God out, I was able to see Him at work in my life.
64. Peace with God is rest.
65. There's conflict on every turn of our adventure towards home, up above, as we journey through God's word the eternal door.
66. Mine eyes have seen the mirror before the word of God, then afterwards His glory looking back at me, for as He spoke I entered in.
67. Life flows out of us when we're talking and walking with God.
68. Count your blessings to know your great value in the sight of God.
69. There is eternal vision when thoughts and emotions are in sync.

70. We must let go of the past and take hold of what God has for us, to grow and possess life for the future.
71. When we see our value in the light of God then we know our true worth.
72. We need protection from what we do not understand so God can teach us what He wants us to understand.
73. Just as Jesus is the word become flesh, when we allow the word of God to become flesh in us, we enter a oneness with the Father and seek to do His will.
74. I do care and I do know, not only will I listen to God, I will obey by asking Him to change me.
75. When people sense you're worth something they'll want to be around you. Know your worth in relation to God, then count your blessings when you're alone.
76. Never take credit for what God does in our lives.
77. Sometimes when we think we're heading in the right direction, then the Holy Spirit redirects us back to God's path.
78. God fills to overflowing those who sing praises to His name continually.
79. I can do nothing, yet not I, it is God who worketh in me to will to do His good pleasure.
80. God will never leave you alone.
81. Do we stand in awe of the soldiers of God, or are we the soldiers people see Jesus in?
82. I love me for who I am and what I'm yet to become by the hand of the great I am.
83. Validate God by believing Him, then the eternal will displace time.
84. With God all is possible, He is astonished at unbelief.
85. God speaks to us, that He is, through all His creations as well as His word.
86. Give that you might behold the giver of all.
87. True fellowship produces life.
88. Jesus is coming soon and yet is even now at the door.
89. Walk so slow, go so slow, that you'll be carried by the Spirit and see forever more.

90. A word spoken in the light brings forth good medicine to those recovering from darkness.
91. Be content with what you have and let God give the increase.
92. There's life in song with understanding that gives God glory.
93. Those made alive walk in the council of God.
94. There's always pain before growth.
95. Wisdom comes from having conscience contact with God, those who dwell here have understanding.
96. Beads of truth connect when we allow God to work in our lives.
97. One touch from Jesus gives life to those in need of an answer.
98. Getting to know God is a collective effort through grace, which grows to give knowledge, of the vision of who He really is.
99. When in doubt wait it out, like a child God will take you by the hand and lead you to where you belong.
100. Whose song are you singing as the notes happen one at a time?
101. Like open nets we collect things from our daily lifestyles. At the end of everyday the conscience that is not clear before God will be troubled, until conscience contact with God is reestablished. God wants us to empty our nets before Him, so we can see how He patiently, gently loves us as we sift, what He already knows is there, what is of the Spirit and ask Him to remove what is not.
102. The treasure of your power which changes death unto life warms my heart with the love of your eternal reality.
103. Grab hold of Jesus and don't let go till He sets you in your place and guides you by His hand.
104. God calls us to read His word and talk with Him throughout the day.
105. Jesus is a divine mandate which lifts us out and sets us apart to serve His reality and no other.

106. When I don't feel so good and things don't go so well, it's nice to have God to go to to comfort me.

107. Drops of water form a puddle, many puddles form a stream, streams form rivers and rivers an ocean such is the Spirit of God with men who partake   of   His relationship.

108. To see God is to know you're not alone.

109. Should you sin wait for God to direct your path.

110. The beauty of believers is connected by the same, the Holy Spirit of God.

111. Nothing has more value than an open door to the eternal and its life.

112. Trust God to change you through grace.

113. Without Christ there is night and too many days of change, for without sunshine the eye adjusts to a different kind of light, the kind that produces dragons.

114. In Christ we have peace, in the world trouble.

115. What is birthed in darkness will grow to choke out the light we need for life.

116. We need to examine our past with the light of God for more life.

117. Our position in life will line up with what we practice.

118. We live by linking God's truth together, know God and live.

119. When love is brought into light there is growth, for without love man cannot face himself.

120. Do not touch the fruit on your tree or any other, be brave and trust Christ for them to live righteously. Know the fruit, submit and let God give it when the time is right, pick it yourself and eat you'll die.

121. We can't build on who we think we are only on the life Christ has given us.

122. There's a washing that takes place as we partake of that which is alive, God's word His nature divine, learning of Christ the more we read the cleaner the roots get, being translated from glory to glory.

123. Many hearts are revealed through the open door to another world. God's word is that book of life which brings forth eternity, a sure foundation.

124. The farther we grow the more we can see what lay ahead and know already what is behind.

125. When man tries to build according to his way there's no foundation to hold him in place.

126. If we don't have something with love to say than pray for one another and keep death away.

127. Even though I've been trained to get even I must let God have control of my anger.

128. God has wisdom for those who seek to understand Him.

129. When we yield our will to God, His grace breaks the barrier to our control.

130. The timing of man is chaos, of God, peace and order.

131. When God restores someone they're a sight to behold.

132. We enter doors to other worlds, foundationally, we can live in only one eternal one.

133. Royalty comes from the beauty of the cross, Christ crucified, no other price will satisfy this condition.

134. Crying out to God, groaning in His Spirit throughout the day, relieves the pressure from demonic stress and allows life to flow in death's place. Once our path is straight all else snaps into place and gets healed.

135. The only right I have is to go to God for justice, then do what He says.

136. In the midst of our trying to figure the best way out of a crisis God is saying, "Let me have it and then go grow on with your life."

137. We're to expect the unexpected without losing peace or perish in the way.

138. People who charm to cover up are hypocrites.

139. Man is two-faced at his best, but God is faithful and always true.

140. God's word is a messenger from above. It seeks us out and rescues us from other worlds.

141. My boundary lines have fallen in pleasant places, apart from God there is no good thing.

142. I've learned to keep Eternal truths in my heart till the time God would have me to reveal them. I may lack in wisdom and judgement but I don't lack in Jesus who will guide me to the end.

143. Our hope lay ahead, Christ is our valiant warrior.

144. Sometimes we follow God's word not knowing what will happen, but do we have any choice knowing what holds our future?

145. Some people would rather be miserable, believe a lie, than know the truth about the condition they're in. While all the while the gift of life is ready to take misery's place.

146. The more we use our faith the easier it gets to trust God.

147. Things that please our senses at first glance, once understood more perfectly, may be revealed in the Spirit as deadly poison.

148. The devil tries to hide us with thoughts that blind the mind's eye. One word from Jesus breaks the clouds, awakes us from an endless rest and saves us.

149. I will set the Lord always before me that He may remain at the center of my affections.

150. All may appear to be in order but when the King visits unexpectedly are we really being partakers of His divine nature? Does our faith, virtue, knowledge, temperance, patience, godliness, brotherly kindness and love stand in the light of His presence yielding a clear conscience before God?

151. There's beauty in the freedom of being set free from the reality of darkness to enter into the Eternal flame's light. Time has been shattered and the Lord as my sword will slice me a path righteously through to heaven's door to enter peacefully in.

152. Life outside the body of Christ is living hell!

153. Don't seek Jesus for the spectacular for this is darkness. Only the light of love and truth-seeking sets men free.

154. As light rolls back darkness everything gets revealed.

155. Now that you know Jesus talk to Him. Tell Him of all your needs and how thing are going daily, this is life for He cares for you.

156. Growth comes through advancing the Kingdom of God with our daily walk, word and deed, seasoned with grace and the Lord as our friend.

157. To be filled with Eternal light and able to walk in a dark world is life.

158. Don't dispute look towards Jesus and share your life.

159. The devil wants us to exchange fantasy for God's reality and blind our minds.

160. When the mind is blind darkness will grow till Jesus pierces it with His light and establishes His stability.

161. A place of honor without God's blessing is marked for destruction.

162. Those who remain faithful to God will see salvation.

163. Tilling the land and planting is important, despite the tramplings of wild animals and birds eating seed, floods and fire for what is foretold will come to pass.

164. Changed from the end to the beginning before it's too late, the Eternal door disappeared as the mind's eye closed for the body had reached its end.

165. Be patient, wait on the Lord and He will restore what you destroyed when you were in a hurry.

166. Too much talking and not enough listening can limit what we learn.

167. Every poor judgement, every idle thought, word or deed that separated us from God, will become an impenetrable wall causing death. It is my goal to be still so nothing comes between me and a conscience contact with God that I may remain joined to Him, grafted into His tree at all times and have eternal life. John 5:14: behold thou art made whole: sin no more least a worse thing come unto thee.

168. We need to enjoy Christ as a friend life and let the Holy Spirit lead the way.

169. The eyes we look through connect us with time or eternity, death or life, the devil or the eternal flame.

170. We eat what we have an appetite for, but how we eat can take our appetite for Christ away.

171. It is a battle to keep the focus of our realities Christ-centered when all else in the world wants to break the hug of our Father's will.

172. Fresh revelation comes when we turn from our ways and look towards God in the person of Jesus Christ.

173. When the tears from pain are mixed with the right fertilizer it helps the seeds grow. Least they die.

174. There is joy in doing the Father's will and honoring His best plan for our life.

175. Those who have God on their minds continually receive the blessing of His strength.

176. There are obstacles which keep us from being still sometimes to keep us from only hearing the voice of God.

177. We choose who we serve in how we relate to others.

178. Beware of those who reinforce misperceived identities.

179. Talk to the Lord for He has provisions for you.

180. Love connects us to our emotions and lets us out of ourselves by truths which transform.

181. It's not impossible to be part of the whole picture when you're only seeing a piece of it.

182. Any pleasure stolen from outside of God's ways are holes in the soul from which spiritual life seeps out.

183. Birth pains bring forth life.

184. We need to come to a place where we will not deny Christ in word or deed, but do children ever stop learning?

185. It is important to keep going back to the bible to keep its reality fresh and alive in the face of all the unbelief. As God's children we need to eat a little bit of His word everyday to remain healthy.

186. The brighter Christ shines in us the more people will be drawn to Him for life or, do we get out of line of being and start doing and keep them from getting a balanced picture understanding the growth of a relationship with God.

187. Those who recognize the ugliness of sin within themselves can be cleansed by the power of Jesus Christ and made beautiful.
188. Once all the wrinkles have been ironed out we can see Jesus on the other side.
189. Children come back to the nest to be strengthened so they can fly again.
190. Seek to find the Eternal Flame through Jesus, the door, and let the spirit of the living God burn inside you, pointing the way for others.
191. There's alot of fear connected with stepping out into the unknown promises of God, but isn't it more exciting than being dead?
192. If you don't have faith you'll never learn to trust God's ways above your own and see Him work in your life.
193. I always check to see if I've wandered from God's safety the way a small child does when he's learning to walk. His daddy's leg is there to grab so he won't fall.
194. God will slowly lead us up His mountain and unfolds every wrong turn so we can find Him and live life to the fullest.
195. Without absolutes all is confusion.
196. You've got to be ready and feel the need for a change before you'll really reach out in faith for perfect love and truth.
197. Jesus came into the world as a witness as He lived out His life in truth He validated God.
198. Jesus uses us to help others then blesses us with friendships in the light.
199. I have eternal vision and do not doubt that's what is real.
200. We live in a lost and dying world. Jesus is the only way out of it. Call upon Him and be saved from it.
201. When life becomes an ordeal we've to learn to pray our way through, talk to God, not handle life on our own.
202. I put my trust in Christ and He keeps carrying my load.

203. People who have structured lives without God live a lie. Only with God is there order for us to know which way to go next with a vision for peace of mind.

204. People must be taught the difference between good and evil according to the bible so that their eyes may be opened to understand eternal life and live.

205. Love goes wherever its called and abides in truth to light the way to go. It is a walk in perfect peace through all that rages and threatens to move us from a path of life, a relationship with Jesus Christ.

206. As a helpless child I called out to God and He answered me with protecting arms witch hold me close. Over the mountains I'm lifted in towards the land of the living I grow. Above the storms He keeps me warm with newfound strength I continue on.

207. God patiently crosses over from time to eternity by grace through the doorway of Jesus Christ. Only then does reality begin.

208. The darkest hour is always before His light where the sting of death gets removed by resurrection power.

209. Be warned: people who don't have a relationship with Jesus spin a web of lies bending reality, whether aware or not, to believe what is false is a trap. Non-discerning believers fall in it and the devil drains their faith to take their lives. This is an anti-Christ spirit. We must be able to love in earnest, which is to say love the truth that we may have light to see, to pull others from this trap and not get pulled in through misperceptions ourselves.

210. Deep relationships take time to grow. You can't get married on a thread.

211. When people are in spiritual knots they cannot see beyond the coils and are in darkness. It is foolish sight to plan your life blind.

212. Freedom is always brought in blood, for when there's a war someonemust die. A memory of honor holds a King of king's worth.

213. It is necessary to give thanks out or prayer, etc... after taking in the many blessings of God or we break away

from His spiritual flow and stagnate, become stale and a prey for darkness once again.

214. To see what Jesus sees we need to get out of the way of the Father and let Him have full control through His son.

215. The further we grow in a relationship with Christ the more we cansee what He's given us. I am satisfied with His goodness.

216. We were born of a sin nature when Adam disobeyed God.

217. Just as Jesus was taunted to come down from the cross, the Devil tries to move us from our position of resurrected life and its peace.

218. Only one can lead in the dance of life.

219. As I magnify the Lord I become enlarged giving off light as a focal point for people to see the way.

220. The genius of man will go down into the grave while the vision of God will last forever.

221. It's easier to die than to lay down your life one day at a time.

222. When you practice righteousness you can cast out the devil in the charachter of Jesus' name.

223. When structure becomes prison we need to be guided by the spirit.

224. We must forgive and have compassion for people who hurt us, that we don't enter into destructive behaviors and miss the blessing of life.

225. How foolish are kings who laugh at the wind and understand not the eye in the midst of a storm, who scoff at trees which lift their arms up high, and listen not to birds which sing sweet songs.

226. Pollywogs become croaking frogs. Butterflies swoon so colorfully after they're transformed, as larva must eat threads of a garment before it can become a moth. Is there order?

227. Say on creation... spiders don't eat before they taylor their prey.

Great trees outgrow their soil and topple over for lack of root. Rain gives cause for things to grow and can replenish a parched dry land.

Mountains wear down and rocks become sand. A tree must produce flowers before fruits and there are many types of fruit as well as fragrance of flowers. When a bee gets angry and stings it dies. Plants all grow and animals alike to the glory and divine nature of God.

228. There are many kings' tables and many banquet feasts, be careful at whose table you sit at and what you're about to eat. If you are a king consider a feast has great cost, much time and energy. It's always best to be invited to the true King's banquet, who has the biggest table. No matter how many guests are bid there will always be room for you and no lack of food to eat.

229. When a man's inner beauty outshines his outer shell then is He a splendor to behold. And when asked what table you've been eating, for people see you've been satisfied. Tell them the true King's table and invite them as well. For a table large enough for all is the true King's table.

230. A tree in a strong wind is only as mighty as its roots. The better the soil the faster we grow. When bark is torn from a tree bugs can come in and kill it. Without rain we will surely die.

231. Things can't grow when water is frozen. To draw away from love makes us freeze.

232. Particles change when water gets too hot. When we run ahead of His presence life gets too hot to handle and we evaporate.

233. The ocean waves break hard against large rocks. A weak rock quickly becomes sand, but a strong rock can last an eternity. To stay in His presence is to draw strength from it and grow. A true word is a never ending rock.

234. When we stand still enough we can feel the wind of time. Jesus spoke to the wind and it stood still. When

our time ends God's eternal time begins. Only then can we touch God and live.

235. Never let fear keep you from telling the truth.

236. Knowing Jesus as a way of life is more than to know Him as King.
When I look through His eyes I see God's living reality and detach from the lie of the misperceptions of the world.

237. God's spirit of Holy purity parts through the wicked spirits, Jesus now becomes the only way through the spiritual sea of wickedness.

238. A bird cannot fly when its wings are broken. A lion cannot roar when he has no strength. A man cannot sing when his heart has no song.

239. Not being mindful of our destiny is like running through a glass door and never realizing we're bleeding. Outside the presence of Christ you bleed, inside Christ you stop.

240. As soothing lotion is needed to protect our dry hands a place of peace is needed to protect our souls.

241. When I close my eyes, that is my room, I either see Jesus or something else standing in it.

242. Love conquers all when our love is for God. God conquers all when my love is for Him.

243. Taking displays who we are in the world and reinforces that identity.
Giving allows the love of God to flow and reinforces us in Christ.

244. Spiritual creatures distract us through demon powers which keep us from confronting the reality of God.

245. Immortality without vitality is worthless.

246. A bird does not live in the dirt when it can have something better. It builds a nest one twig at a time, and it is unique. Each empty nest tells what kind of bird lived there and to where it has flown. What type of nest are we building, and to where will it show us to have flown?

247. Great is His shelter, mighty is His hand, I am secure in God in Him do I stand.

248. One time my love was for material things for they gave me joy, however, what I loved was sin in the eyes of God. It is a narrow road unto salvation, but I know my tears of letting go will one day turn to joy. To lay down my life is hard to do yet easy in the reality of God.

249. My reigns are being tried as my heart does tear on every snare. I'm learning to surrender then easier becomes my walk. Now I can run with Jesus with the presence of God.

250. I know one day the trumpet will sound and will be heard through all eternity. Oh to feel your still and peaceful presence everyday. I'm home at last.

251. When past objects haunt my mind, I remember the death of its destruction and stand before my savior with no past.

252. My flesh still tries to fight me down as I try to hold on to my way.

Then I am mindful of my master the King. I am weak in the greatness of His name. All the secret places of my heart are brought to remembrance by the complete freedom of His breath and all His ways.

253. There was a time when I cried with no place to go. I'm so glad there's a King who hears, this does cause my heart to sing.

254. Tree of life, your spirit does glisten and flow. It sparkles so brightly as it quenches my thirsts. Oh Lord Jesus your word is first. I am still and wait for you to move me as I drink.

255. Oh my Strong Mountain that caresses with love. You are watching over me. I feel your presence wherever it is that I do go.

256. Love - takes growth and is understood by its depth over time in that it builds relationships.

Lust - takes what it can get, when it can get it showing no regard for others, only thinking of itself.

257. God almighty has all power at His command for the asking. When man tries to reach in and take what is not his to call power his own he'll get death instead of life.

258. To live for God is to be strong and free. To live for self, our wants and desires, is to step into the mouth of hell.

259. God is joy even in the midst of pain. Prayer is to see God at all times.

260. When we obey God's voice, to not give in to the lusts of the flesh, and let go by grace of the misperceptions of the world, it is possible to grow on into a deeper relationship with God. We are carried to safety as God walks us through.

261. I close my eyes and I can see Him. I lift my arms and I can touch Him.
When I open my mouth my words reach Him. I serve Jesus because He is alive and I love Him.

262. In the midst of my troubles I continued to look unto my Lord and all became quiet.

263. No not one can stand in the light of your presence my King of Glory except it be by grace.

264. When the enemy tried to follow I turned looking to you all the more my Lord and you sustained me in the midst of the heat.

265. America is losing its Godly heritage, through godless entertainment and education. This country is slowly going blind.

266. Children only behave when parents stand still trusting God to judge them by their walk. God roots things out of us through our children. The faults we find in others we usually don't see within ourselves.

267. Beware of fast lived thoughts in the mind without actions steadfast in Jesus Christ to back them up.

268. When the very flames of hell beat about the reality of a living God, look neither to the left or the right. When doubt tries to breach you and pride, confess your fainting straight way to the Lord and your honest cry will lift to the right hand of God's throne with a kiss.

269. Kiss the Lord with the love of a heart full of yearning. Then he'll bare the weight of your load and slay all that oppress you till they come no more. By standing on God's word we're shaped facing the winds of time.

270. Keep me in a full measure of your presence. Guide my steps and still my tongue, so I may rest in your love all the days of my life.

271. As a ripple on a still lake, words of peace should never react or all peace is lost.

272. It is by our own choice we put Christ to death regardless of what influences us.

273. Whoever Jesus touches speaks righteously.

274. There is growth when all earthly worldly distractions are removed from the path of God. All affections, attractions, or any other self-seeking pleasure or indulgence must be removed by the blood of Jesus Christ, as revealed to us, we ask for a clear conscience which brings change.

275. Keep your banners up, every victory won by Christ keeps the enemy away for they shine bright as a noon day sun.

276. The Holy word of God does not lie; it satisfies. Thanks be unto God for His indescribable gift, the taste is sweeter than anything I know.

277. Just as Noah built an ark and people mocked him, we must build a relationship with God no matter what others say about us.

278. Moses broke the ten commandments. God must build them in our hearts. The broken pieces were carried around in an ark, something God designed, which man had to choose to build with his own free will.

279. The more we know of Jesus and the less of ourselves the wider the door to God's presence becomes.

280. Our words are like a well-tailored suit, they fit us and let people know what we are wearing, who we are. Our words cannot be worn everywhere and end when we die. God's word, the bible, is the finest tailored suit. There's not one thread out of place, every word holds true.

Through Jesus Christ we are able to give the devil back his suit and put on an eternal one. Worn in the gutter and in front of kings this suit can be worn anywhere, with no embarrassing spots of nakedness in it.

281. Shining in joy its the tingling sensation of His love divine. It's praise beyond victory, praise beyond me, it's heavenly places that's what I see.

282. No matter what my misperceptions tell me I know you are there. I'll never forget the battles you fought from reality to glory and won for me. Jesus grows from the inside out to others and adds to Himself.

283. The life-giving light of Jesus sparkles in eyes in the midst of darkness and gets God's attention. Each cry for help produces more life and grows us further in to the Father's presence.

284. Let go! and God will fill you. There's hope for anyone who puts their trust in God.

285. Whenever I feel the pain of my ways I always remember my tears don't answer me and reach out to a Christ who always does.

286. As blind children we stumble into God's presence. "Teach us to seethe way to go to cause us no more pain."

287. When you are standing still the world will notice Jesus.

288. I am just like a candle, Jesus is the flame. When the devil tries to blow it out we always interpret the wind.

289. When my heart talks instead of Christ I always lose my way. Then I see His light saying, "Come to me. All is forgiven. Don't be shy. I'll see you through." "Continue your relationship with me."

290. Jesus looks on all those who suffered the pains and chains of this life.

He watches as we draw closer to obtain comfort and a greater understanding of His presence. The physical pains of the cross was bad but the rejection of His loving us, I understand as I draw closer too.

291. In comprehending Jesus we understand the pain of loving with no one to give to, and hated for the love we have at the same time.

292. One who has truly come to the cross must have "Father forgive them for they know not what they do," pierced in the heart.

293. God's love before selfish desires unites us.

294. The closer I get to Jesus the greater the revelation of salvation from Hell's destructive damnation, an eternal, ever-increasing knowledge of pain, I am set free from.

295. Lord Jesus your great light shows me my nakedness, I am blind as to a way to even clothe myself. All I'm learning to say is be merciful and clothe me, my God and my friend.

296. Trust God to bring you all the way and wait on Him to do it.

297. God is patient and merciful for He will not let me see what I'm not ready to see. Oh the glory of His love, His hand is holding mine.

298. The flame of your great love burns inside, there is no place left to hide.
All is open like a book, people see this when they look. Have the memories all faded? Have I truly been set free? I search my heart before you, I am still now that I see.

299. With soul-tickling laughter the beauty of your presence Lord Jesus is truly beyond words. You came into my prison and broke down all the walls, now I'm brand new and free to praise and worship you.

300. Hold your ground and be confident in what you know about God and mountains will be moved. Peace will then stand where chaos once ruled.

301. All my thoughts were dark, now they fight against the light in the renewing of my mind.

302. Imagination fights against our minds and tries to prevent revelation with anything it can conjure up to distract us.

303. Just as the Holy Spirit overshadowed Mary, when we believe, it overshadows us birthing a new creation in us. This work grows to be Christ in us, from an eternal seed of faith.

304. It may look right, feel right, things may even line up to say it's right, but if the peace of the Spirit of God is not there flee for destruction awaits you.

305. When Jesus talks at all times life becomes looking through His eyes and a crusade.

306. Unity in the Bond of Peace joined through all and in all. It is this thread that holds us and with its power restores all. It is the Prince of Peace who justly rules over all.

307. I'm in tune with why reality is always growing. I'm happy Christ gave it to me.

308. There is a timing where all will fit together orderly as we trust God and surrender our control.

309. We are linked to eternity from thought to thought. Whatever breaks this link diverts our focus from God. It is only by grace we are drawn back from time continually.

310. When cutting a dotted line, when the dots don't line up, we can never go straight through to the other side.

311. The more power we think we have the less room for faith there is to bring life.

312. A deeper walk with Jesus occurs when our thoughts and emotions are woven into the eternal reality of God to the point where we outgrow ourselves, knowing Christ only.

313. Some people have a one-sided relationship with God and don't know how to respond to Him, being set in their ways they need to read His word and ponder, (chew His flesh), to be able to enjoy Him as life with all His blessings.

314. Blessings are everywhere but how slow we are to recognize them.

315. How we view God will determine the outcome of our prayer life.

316. People who are always looking for something really are looking to escape death.

317. We protect our children by living by the standard of Biblical truth which promotes no moral decay, righteousness holds back the floodgates of hell, as God goes before all generations.

318. We strut about proud feeling oh so strong till something goes wrong.
Only in the light of Jesus can we see how frail we really are. It is here we ask for help and through His grace are changed from death unto life.

319. When all is at its darkest and no hope can be found, it takes a word to Jesus and the prison walls crack, then crumble and come a tumbling down.

320. The Lord is my strength, all of my righteous actions are done by Him.

321. A spider has the ability to create its own world but moves on when no food enters into its web.

322. His word is law, help will come, I trust Jesus and His promises as a ray of breakthrough faith, help has just arrived.

323. People who settle for less than the prize, miss, life everlasting.

324. With all misperceptions there's a spiritual malnutrition which causes the mind's eye to go dim. Only a steady daily diet of prayer and reading God's word will keep it clear and in contact with the eternal light of Jesus Christ.

325. Maintaining conscience contact with God through Christ is eternal life.
Knowing Jesus only as He walks and lives and breathes, we in Him.

326. Judgement brings condemnation and cuts off love, beware of preconceived ideas.

327. Jesus breaks the chains of generational sins and sets us free to worship Him.

328. Jesus could only do what He saw His father doing as He is in us watch and pray for what to do next each moment of everyday.

329. There's no need to care what other people think when our eyes are on Jesus.

330. To search out God is to accept Him on His terms and rejoice with new life.

331. The day I got saved I watched that night, with open closed eyes, the demons screamed as they could not get

back in. Their nails scratched the walls as they slid away into oblivion.

332. We're to stand in what we know of the way, and cry out to Jesus when we've reached its end.

333. Go your way and sin no more, forgiveness sets the captive free.

334. It's important to belong to a body of Christ, it takes more than one drop to make a river, each drop reinforces the others.

335. As God does pray through us power for creation takes place, our words become His words in agreement which brings forth life.

336. With Jesus time stands still and eternity is experienced as it is real.

337. When we spill dirt it spreads around.

338. Just hold on to me and trust and I will see you through.

339. Whenever dark thoughts creep into our minds to steal our precious life remember Jesus is the light of the world.

340. We're all apart of a family but are we aware of if it's where we want to belong.

341. You can't look at someone with eyes of love when judgement is in the way.

342. Trees don't move, they spread their arms and drink in rays of light from the sun.

343. Nothing is done in darkness that is not seen by light.

344. There's a beauty in every child of God which surpasses our own understanding and brings tears of joy to the eye.

345. When we think we're okay usually we're not, we always need God's guidance.

346. We don't have to talk we can let Christ speak through us.

347. Once having partaken of eternal life the things of time lose their flavor.

348. Tongues break our conscience contact with the reality of time and join us with eternity and its reality.

349. Those who don't sing to God sing a miss and those listening are in danger of missing His will.

350. Luck says things just happen but blessings are forever.

351. People cry years of tears, lost at sea they are, how few seem to make it to the shore for the answer to return for more.

352. It is better to die serving the Lord than to live through the lie of a life without Him.

353. The accomplishments of the flesh are death whereas the spirit love and life.

354. When I make a mistake I plead the blood of Jesus to cleanse me and correct the damage. Then I'm redeemed to continue on with a full king's worth coheir to the throne of God.

355. What makes a king is knowing the truth which sets us apart from darkness and on high lifted up with Jesus.

356. It takes time to be seen for who we are for peace stands still to fast-paced eyes and is different as is eternity.

357. The devil tries to distract us from Jesus with a swirl of his own thoughts planted in our minds, but eternity will always break all the sands of time.

358. It's a sad world when children don't listen to their parents who speak the truth in love to light their way.

359. When love clears the window to the mind's eye, open it up and let life, eternal truth in.

360. It is good to dwell on the blessings of God for they produce joy, gladness to the heart for long life.

361. Those who imitate Adam will hold no life just as those who imitate Christ will be filled.

362. People have to learn of and experience a relationship with God for themselves, however; there are catalysts which serve as examples and aid or hinder in this process.

363. As children we want to grow up to understand all the answers of life.
    As adults we long to be children so that we can trust in the comfort of someone taking care of us. God looks on all the while wanting to give us both.

364. The more we give our trust to God the more room we have for God's spirit to fill us and give life through us.

365. We need to come to a place, that wherever we're at God's word will meet us, keeping us in contentment always as we follow Him.

366. God's power doesn't let someone off the hook it sets them free to give and receive His love forever.

367. The devil tries to get us to act out on our best choices so he can possess us, rather than consult God the way to life and lose us.

368. We need to read the word of God and pack our minds until all we see is God, the knowledge of His grace.

369. If you don't know who you are, how are you going to find your way to where you belong?

370. When love is the tree its fruits are sweet. Love gives without expecting anything in return.

371. In prayer, there's a wrestling that takes place till we find our peace. Prayer is like eating a meal. Waiting on God is the appetizer, entering into His presence is steak, and all the glorious talk is dessert. Prayer is like climbing a mountain. We start at its base and become elevated to its heights.

372. Direction has balance when prayer leads to reading God's word and reading God's word leads back to prayer.

373. The foundations of old is laid through all generations and grows eternally bigger. Our hope links us through any dark hour and keeps our focus on the light of Christ.

374. Jesus Christ. He has healed my mind. He is therefore I am, I am therefore He is.

375. It's not about us knowing it all, it's about us knowing Jesus Christ.

376. God works on relationships by getting us to focus on ourselves with Himself before us. Then as we grow closer to Him we draw closer to others   as   well. Relationships are healed when God is at the center, instead of seeing old hurts we see God's character and then the walls come down around us.

377. Jesus always reflected His Father's will, in that while we were yet sinners, He has His Father's compassion

and takes our place. He suffers for us, that we may be free to move into a relationship with the living loving I and the Father are one God.

378. God's love controls us when we truly receive God's love, we will become loving.

379. It is important to maintain conscious contact with your children throughout their lives, know them each day, so they'll know Christ's love in you rather than bond with the darkness of this world.

380. A sign of spiritual strength is the joy of the Lord. When in step with God we always have peace. We will always have peace and be bonded to the unity of His love. With the many uncertainties in life it's nice to know there's a God who holds for us a certain future.

381. We must learn to see the flags of a person's character before, as we join in a relationship with them, without losing sight of Christ.

382. Camping out in places too long can cause us to miss the voice of the Lord when it's time to move on.

383. To be afraid of the unknowingness of the dark is not to be looking at the light of Christ.

384. Only the provisions of God are real, all else, say "It isn't real", calling on the name of the Lord and it will disappear. It isn't real if it isn't You Lord Jesus such as is eternal life.

385. God is always on time......but without His timing we continually hurt ourselves. Lord I need to be consciously aware of You moment by moment and our life together to avoid such hurt, amen.

386. Sex outside of marriage is a lie which leads to destruction.

387. How tall would a tree grow if it kept on jumping around; it would have to keep starting over, thus limiting growth.

388. Authority comes from God who is the light in this darkened world.

389. People won't recognize the body of Christ until it moves as one with Christ.

390. People are not going to understand what you try to tell them unless you patiently wait for them to give you their good ear. It takes just as much faith to believe a lie as it does the truth.

391. God takes us from banging our heads against the walls to encountering His riches.

392. A shaky foundation produces an unstable mind.

393. When we are filled with love and truth life will flow to others. It's not the words, I'm sharing through His life in me which becomes life to others everywhere I acknowledge Him.

394. We carry Christ in us wherever we go, we must let out what's inside to let others reflect, do people notice His life shining forth when they see us, to wake them from their enchanted sleep or are we dim.

395. Do we see or do we think we see, knowing Jesus is forever.

396. When there's no one to show us the way uncertainty looms over us at every turn. Everything in God's time, light will come.

397. You must touch Jesus knowing He's alive to enter in beyond the veil.

398. Both blessings and cursings are present in our daily walk, best be aware how we conduct our affairs.

399. Just as bread goes stale, we also, if we're not feeding off of God's word, the bread of life daily.

400. A true relationship with God, (Love + Truth = Light), is deeper than time and more satisfying increasingly to all the senses. Learn of Him and you'll live forever. His invitation stands, "Learn of Me I want to know you that you'll know what it is to know completely."

401. If we respect God we respect one another as living souls whom God created and loves, everyone grows at different rates.

402. In sharing Christ through the way we live our lives in Him, we rescue members of His royal family. Unknowingly or knowingly we are sent royally forth each day.

403. God carries us at times through each other.

404. Life is a journey which becomes changed when we trust God to hold our future. Standing still in His ways can be a battle.

405. When God's word pierces me through my soul becomes pregnant with life, then come the voices of darkness to try to kill it and put out the light, with its illusions, showing what is off balance as the real world.

406. When life becomes a labor of love we find ourselves enmeshed with God and observe the spectacle of serving eternity and eternal life.

407. Self-seeking people are off balance and bring confusion, they will never know God's order of peaceful growth unless they come to know, "The time is fulfilled, and the Kingdom of heaven is at hand: repent ye, and believe God's word." Come enter in and join us.

408. We're being prepared through confession and repentance growing insights, a revelation of Christ's righteousness, into our souls.

409. As a broken bone is set by a cast for healing, a break in the spirit must be set back into place by the word of God, when applied correctly.

410. Born an illegitimate child set against the spirit of God, Jesus found me and took me in with the price of His life. He washed me with His own blood and bore me with His spirit, fed me with His word. I no longer belong to the world, now I belong to the family of God.

411. Winds may dance about the flame but it is God's grace which keeps the candle from going out.

412. When we think we've got it all together, how helpless we must look in God's eyes, full of compassion.

413. When I close my eyes at night there's nothing between me and my God, I enjoy this peace. Jesus said, "If I be lifted up from the earth I will draw all men unto me." Let's enjoy Jesus in each other while being made perfect and already are perfected in Him.

414. Jesus spoke the word of God with authority for that is who He is, and He's always speaking through it.

415. When we camp, share, or dance around the great fire, which strengthens us, singing of what we know of God's word and keep on adding to its reality it burns brighter still in us and in those around us. It directs our lives as it gives us eternal fire for life, this is the living flame which consumes all else.

416. May the fire of God's invited flame which came in through Christ Jesus our Lord that entered within you burn brighter than the flames that surround you. The dark fire cannot withstand the spirit of the living God. Speak out light in love and truth and live forevermore.

417. Everytime we wrong someone it is Jesus we're hurting. He suffered the cross that we may go free, as long as we repent and receive His forgiveness.

418. We're to look through the eyes of Jesus and see the empty people who want to get filled.

419. A learned behavior of distant love, (love without intimacy from mother and father), will marry us to religion and rob us of a relationship with God.

420. When we push God out of our lives it hurts Him. He feels the rejection of His love towards us.

421. Though mother and father or even children or else forsake thee for my namesake. I the Lord your God shall bear thee up.

422. When we look beyond the perfect mirror of God's word our reflection disappears as we see His light in us, reality can be found here, the kind that brings forth life.

423. The distance or separation between two people is as close as their faith.

424. Misperceiving reality we get into the kind of trouble only God can get us out of.

425. With each new day of growth I can never run out of reasons for giving God praise.

426. At the throne of grace I need to take God more seriously and know He will work His character in me.

427. Don't get so predetermined about seeking God as to not meet Him.

428. As by grace we cry out to Your eternal shore; the tide of time is always against us. It is here we pass to where temptation's death of this world no longer has hold of our life and its dark sting gives way to Your peace, from the beauty of Your light. God wants us to honor His word above all else so that we may be citizens (joint heirs) in His Kingdom and His fellow doors which live by faith standing one day at a time. God cannot lie; those who believe Him through faith and patience they inherit the promise, His order, which is to say eternal life.

429. The whole earth is under an evil enchantment which puts minds to sleep and dulls the senses; dark fire which brings discontentment. It is the heat of the unfulfilled desire which burns the life out of us producing no light for direction and no growth. It's hell's gateway, through broken expectations and demands what we think we have hold of becomes sand, lies slipping through our fingers. Only the eternal flame satisfies through spontaneous love as when the angel of the Lord came upon the shepards in the field and the glory of God shown round about them as angels proclaimed the birth of Christ, this love grows and fills with life. When truth is constant everything that lines up with it, Jesus, will become our constant and enters into the light of eternity this breaks the devil's enchantment forever, amen.

430. Ps 69:7,8... For your sake I have borne reproach; shame has covered my face. I have become a stranger to my brothers, and an alien to my mother's children... God's thoughts in our mind gives us His consciousness, His word become flesh in us and a link with His reality which we can talk through, making us strangers to the reality of this out-of-order world. Our train of thinking has become straight, in order, to use wisdom on how to respond to the needs of those who won't recognize our sanity. ...Ps 69:9 Because zeal for your house has eaten me up, and the reproaches of those who reproach you have fallen on me.

431. God builds His church, He directs man as the over sheppard as High King.

432. Only the Holy Spirit can speak to us about sin. To try to bend someone else's will to agree with us is witchcraft. We must seek to understand people and pray, not to be understood for ourselves for this will happen in our revelations of others through Christ.

433. When our problems become bigger than life with Christ then death will enter in and rob us of our heritage in the eternal.

434. And a great multitude of people went out to meet Jesus and I as one of them pressed through and touched Him to become restored, made whole.

435. God loves us enough to let us make our own mistakes in life, so that we may learn of our own relationship with Him. We truly come to Him when we run out of the reality of our own way. It is here we meet the cross and follow becoming woven into the fabric of His eternal ways which then become ours.

436. As the plow is drawn by oxen so the Spirit of God draws my soul; it breaks the soil of misperceptions of the world and plants seeds of righteousness, as they spring up they yield eternal life. If the plow blade becomes dull it drags and will not cut to bring conviction. I'm learning more about God's perceived conscience through the redemptive power of Jesus Christ, which sharpens as it leads the way out of this dark lost world. I know God can be with me all at all time, but my mind doesn't match the reality of me being with Him in an even exchange of thoughts. It is reflection on God's actions and words which renew the mind. "Be with me and I will be with you."

437. I've been broken before God to see His better plan that I may follow where He leads.

438. After meeting Him we are to keep our eyes on Him with conscience contact above all else for Jesus is the author and finisher of our faith; Christ states we're to be

focused in agreement with Him as one and collectively apart of the same loving body.

439. Too much learning too fast can distort your relationship with Jesus making it off balance and a lie.

440. There's joy in growing at God's pace and we're becoming like Him, when Jesus is standing all around us we're heading in the right direction.

441. I am convinced all fighting takes place outside of the reality of a relationship with Jesus Christ.

442. The name of Jesus is above every other name and any requests made in Its faithfullness climbs as the resurrection above all else gaining access to the throne of God.

443. By being silent and focusing on Jesus we'll be ready to hear the good news God has for us.

444. If we serve God out of love then we're free from sin.

445. One man and God make a majority.

446. God is my friend He stays by my side when the hard times come and encourages my song, His love for me is always brand new.

447. Comfort zones are war zones to the Spirit where only change will take place when God outshines their darkness.

448. We go into battle standing still full of Christ in us.

449. I want to be an example of the love of God.

450. Praising God changes our feelings. Time with God will lift our spirits.

451. Our lives are lived out of a response to God.

452. People are ready to do for God but are they ready to spend time with Him?

453. God wants us to serve Him by having a relationship with Him.

454. Jesus Christ is the only standard we should allow to come along side to compare ourselves to.

455. Jesus I need you in my life always.

456. God is not way out there He's way in there in us so that the world may know Him in a relationship with us.

457. Let God your friend out of you to draw closer to Him and that others may come to know Him too.

458. I've been accepted by God through the blood of Jesus Christ His Son.

459. My life is continually in my hands but I do not forget your ways, oh Lord, no I do not forget your ways.

460. We can't work our way to heaven, we only need to come to Christ.

461. We must be aware God is with us for Him to be our friend.

462. As we stand on God's word we get changed by the friction from the advancing armies.

463. Search out God's word and get wisdom, live in wisdom and get understanding which keeps us wise.

464. The only way to be Godly is to have the God Christ inside of us. It is this Jesus we invite into our lives who gently teaches the way to live Godly when we allow Him to.

465. Spiritual warfare takes place when we're tempted to choose an illusion in place of the truth.

466. Mercy granted is a covering of comfort for the soul and a seat of hospitality.

467. It is necessary to rest in God's order to trust He's in control and God of your life.

468. When realities clash God wants us to bring our problems to Him and wait for Him to iron them out and solve them.

469. When we no longer have faith in our own abilities we're ready to have faith in God and to trust Him in all our affairs.

470. We're to let out our words before God and justice will prevail.

471. By the shed blood of Jesus Christ, by this grace of the Lord our God is our protector and our keeper.

472. Seeing Jesus with the heart, mind and soul heals the body of its dark works, allows for spiritual growth, and lays all to rest in blessed assurance.

473. God is perfect His order guides us, when we try to hold on to perfection we let go of Jesus and His power to change. We are helpless, we don't know what's going to happen from one moment to the next.

It's all by grace we're held in position, only God is our rock an everlasting word who holds it all together. Anything that suggests we stand or are in control beware of, it isn't you but a lie. We cannot perfect our old natures we can as God's children only let Christ renew us.

474. We're continually building bridges while feasting in the Kingdom of God, yet not us but Christ who is in us, to a lost and dying world.

475. Quiet times alone with Jesus makes us sensitive to what is not of Him.

This prepares us to stand in Him, perfect peace, in the heat of battle of the time based world which will only always cave in to eternal truth.

476. We must study something new looking through God's eye to examine it closely, very carefully, before allowing it to be applied to our lives or we'll be filled with the falsehoods of assumption, everything that feels good is okay.

477. When the barns are full and there's still plenty to harvest it is time to give out the gift of life, before you drink more knowledge of the Master. We overflow by grace till taking and giving become one and the same. Only Jesus can do this!

478. Everything outside the reality of Jesus Christ is an illusion which leads down into the pit.

479. Only the truth can fill the space which restores order to unlock our lives to receive God's love which moves with peace about the soul.

480. We seek which gives God pleasure; by faith God invites us as a gift by grace into a relationship which yields a new identity and a reality of order.

481. When I triumph over a problem, it's not I but Christ which dwells within me; I just thank Him and receive

the joy of His presence, for I...I am the one that He did choose, the same as He did you.

482. Behind every lie there's an advancement of the kingdom of darkness.

The truth will always force it out retaining life in its place.

483. "But I say unto you who soever looks upon a woman with lust already commits adultery with her in his heart."

Our fleshly unrenewed mind thoughts betrays us, to deny this is to get dragged down into the pit.

God's love enables us to see our sinful condition and a need for us to call upon Jesus, our ever-present help in time of need. When led of the Spirit we will not fulfill the lusts of the flesh.

484. As the Spirit moves me grace covers me with the love of God which embraces my soul and holds me deep from within my inner being.

Chords are struck and the song begins; Jesus Christ is in me oh joyful joy. A storm arises all becoming unsettled, I wrestle with my own destructive abilities. Then I remember my song Jesus is the one who called to me and it is Jesus who'll work out His salvation in me, my inheritance, my testimony, my redeemer, in Him I am set free. In God's presence it's alright to be me with my flaws. It is His Kingdom power in me which releases me from satan's claim on me.

Glory to the King! "Greater is He that is in me than he that is in the world."

485. People want a place to land to reaffirm who they are and where they are. Hear out a matter before you pass judgement.

486. God's word, or the lack thereof, sets the course for our hearts to follow. The real Jesus sets us free to experience peace and love and joy, we're made right with God and these are His fruits.

487. When our plans or viewpoints get interrupted, rather than try to figure out everything ourselves, that which is out of reach surrender to God.

He will carry out the best plan, a plan of love for us for He will work it in us and bring it to pass.

488. Be aware we are always sinners and that the love of God, which allows us to believe on Jesus, is God's grace which saves us from being slaves to sin. It is key to remember mercy triumphs over judgment. We're forgiven, let God love you, Jesus works all of our flaws into the fabric of life for good. Substance has compassion; this knowledge leads to an ever-expanding increasing grace. This keeps our relationship with God fresh as we recognize Him at work in us, in our lives daily. I've grown to know God is always there for us to look upon all the time, in the now. With trusting in self out of the picture we'll bond as one with Gods interests, His sanity, and not mans at heart. In our yielding we become objective, we allow Christ to become our subjectivity. Seeing through to where Christ leads to lost souls and beyond our struggles to where we're going to grow, us with Christ, not alone. Serving Jesus in Jesus; to trust that He will train us keeps us spontaneously free, there's only grace and its peace here, fellowship with Jesus forevermore- amen.

489. Jesus reached out with compassion and slowly, layer upon layer, healed my hurts till He touched my inner core and made me whole. He continues to keep me whole daily as my center now revolves around Him, though I may drift; I always return to stand in His peace. His true self, having absolute eternal identity order, to be coppied for a healthy love and truth filled enjoyable life which sets a standard for all those who admitt they need one.

490. **Survival:** A) Without salvation through Christ people just survive on lines and in relationships as they restlessly try to be patient through their frustrations of disorder, they inadequitly get their needs met; they survive life instead of enjoying the gift of it. How does one come to rely on God rather then survive? It is a matter of learning to be honest with our power for

creation for healthy growth, right actions and words reveal to us who we seek by faith. In survival we judge everything and everybody for the protection of our self centeredness. As apart of the body of Christ we're protected by God and filled with His love in judgements place.

We must be aware of our forgiveness of sins and that we've been saved by grace in order to be apart of one body; that the world may see us thrive spiritually and in unity. We are learning how to rely on God and not survive with our own self centered devices, one problem at a time. This builds a relationship with God with a trust He's alive.

B) Having a survival mentality drives us into the religion of self and keeps us from Gods love relationship with emotional unavailability towards others as well. Survival says to obey God through honoring the law, which is to say works, (survive your way to heaven). It does not understand the language of the gift of grace which speaks of trust, peace and love to take survivals place. Nor does it know how to be filled to reap loves benifits which truly satisfy. It's an insane deception which feeds the very pride of lifes' flame, (to separate us further from God), gotta make it on my own, my own strength gets ingrained or drilled into us for so long we don't even know it's there. Unfortuneately we listen to this voice rather than accept the covering of Almighty Gods' invincible strength through Jesus Christ. It is here we start to learn of Gods order along with His sanity.

Survival comes from fear out of lack of trust for God to provide. Have we forgotten or learned how to trust Gods way over our own through faith in Jesus Christ by prayer; the way Jesus prayed to His Father in His trials. Jesus didn't survive on His own He relied on His Father without drifting away from His own love + truth = light reflected nature.

C) People rule kingdoms to survive and neglect their own children who grow to become survivors, insanity gets perpetnated. This should not be the case, for to serve Gods Kingdom fullfills all the requirements to life and saves the land. I want the light of Jesus for life, not the dark fire of survival in the valley. As children of God we trust and follow our Father whose the giver of life. Now inside the body of Christ we're no longer in our own niche which contains no bond of love or lasting abiding joy. Through faith in Christ we've all, for Jesus is our all in all. I've learned we survive to cover up fears, insecurities of being alone and imcomplete; so we put up a front not to face them. God wants us to give up surviving 'the fight', being judgemental with our own light and other things that keep people away, or attract unhealthy people towards us. God wants us to trade them in for intamacy with Himself, through the person of Jesus Christ, that we may be preciously beautiful and free. Now with the agenda for survival out of the way we're able to start practicing humility, the process of emptying self that we may be available for God to use. Now I'm eternally alive with Christ in me guiding me, without even knowing it sometimes, to tell others about Himself. If you'd like please pray,

> Lord I need to see the way to your shore. I want to be apart of your world. I know Jesus died for my sins, the best I know how I claim your promise and thank you for my new life. Thank-you Jesus, Thank-you Jesus, Thank-you Jesus.

If when you've prayed this prayer you did not enter into Gods reality, pray it over and over again till you enter in. You can thank Jesus as many times as you like, look in the mirror at your eyes. Can you see the change, if not

keep praying. Read your Bible every day your soul
needs good spiritual food. Grow in Peace.

Respectfully,

R.A. Feller

P.S. If you're struggling.
First we must realize life is a gift before we can ask the
giver of it how it operates properly. I will guide those
with mine eye, who choose to trust to follow me.

Walking With Jesus In His Service

Eph, 5:14 wherefore He sayeth, Awake though that sleepest, and arise from the dead, and Christ shall give thee light. After I received my gift of salvation my eyes were opened to the sin natures of myself and those around me. My sexual partners skieved me to where my skin crawled. My homosexual partner took time to break away from, but I finally saw him, darkness as with all sin, and what they are, rotting flesh with maggots all over its body, as with all sin it devours. Then I realized they were crawling on me as well, and I felt the pain of my bondage. With my spiritual eye I saw my life getting sucked out of me. Even in the very act Christ showed me how helpless I was and that it would be by believing on Him and nothing else I was to be set free. Finally I took a stand, as I burned I believed and then I became His child prize, the maggots were gone, and I rejoiced in the company of His love. Jesus had set me free and I became clean. I tried to express myself to Charles how the love of God through Christ was sweet, better than what the lust of the flesh had to offer but he wouldn't listen to me and a few years later he killed himself. As for told by Jude 18...there should be mockers in the last time, who should walk after their own ungodly lust.

Christ filled up my life, His word replaced my thoughts and His spirit my direction. John chapter 14: 12, 13, 14 Verily, verily, I say unto you, he that believeth on me, the works that I do shall he do also; and greater works than these shall he do; because I go unto my Father. And whatsoever ye shall ask in my name, that will I do, that the Father may be glorified in the son. If ye shall ask anything in my name, I will do it.

God set me free now I wanted to tell other people about what He did for me He could do for them as well, God can meet your needs through Jesus Christ. I ministered among the homeless proclaiming the good news about how Christ called me out of the world system and gave me eternal life in its place. Eph 6:15 see then that ye walk examining yourselves, not as fools but as wise. I had become filled with eternal life and it was now Christ I shared.

One girl in her twenties, I'd say, who I spoke with about Jesus had just lost her baby. She confessed she neglected her baby for a heroin addiction and had a look like a light bulb that had just blown out. A man standing next to me heard her say she was hungry and would like a bologna and cheese sandwich. I just said flat out, "Can I pray with you?" She eagerly agreed and I led her. "Jesus I need you in my life, come into my heart and fill me with your spirit," from my best recollection, and she lit up like a 100 watts into her bulb, she beamed with light. Grinning from ear to ear, as she was, I offered her some bible literature. She tried to take it but her arm was swollen with infection and she couldn't even close her hand. Then I felt led of the spirit and I took her arm and started to lift it, I heard a voice inside my head say unto me, "She's a brand new Christian. You don't want to lose her." But my reply was, "Let us see what the Lord will do." I raised her arm above her shoulder saying, "In the name of the Lord Jesus Christ ye be healed."

Instantly the swelling ran through her arm, up into her hand and then out through her fingertips into thin air. Unknown to me there were other homeless people watching who were also touched. When the man returned with the sandwich he couldn't believe it was the same girl. Then one of the homeless people stepped forward and said, "You should listen to this man." He just gave her the sandwich and went away scared shouting, "You hypnotized her." The devil had duped his mind.

The next thought that hit me was whose next. I found a youth around nineteen. He had been struck by a car. It bumped his knee and now he walked with a cane and a limp. I approached him and told him that Jesus could heal him if he put his trust in Him. I prayed with him and he received Christ. Then I told him to walk thanking Jesus. At first nothing happened, but I just told him to keep thanking Jesus as he walked hobbling in a circle. All at once his leg shifted into position and he started to jump up and down shouting with joy, then he threw away his cane saying I don't need this anymore. Unfortunately he followed me around saying, "You're an angel" till I was finally able to convince him otherwise.

I came across a homeless woman sitting in the Port Authority who had an eye that was dry and looked cracked. I had compassion for her. I went into a nearby store, wet a napkin and went over to her. She was despondent and I wiped the damp napkin, moved with compassion, over her eye slowly saying, "In the name of the Lord Jesus Christ be healed" and after I removed the napkin from her eye it was completely restored. Later that evening a few hours later I saw her drinking a beer within a crowd of other drunks. She said she didn't want to talk, but that was okay. The fact that her eye was still healed would continue to do all the talking she needed.

I became transparent and would always allow Jesus to have His way with me, whenever street witnessing I'd fast that my flesh would not get in the way. Under the influence of the Holy Spirit I was able to lead many to Christ, such as a crack addict who cursed me at first, but not being able to resist God's spirit, kissed me after receiving Christ being set free. Jude 21,22,23 keep yourselves in the love of God, looking for the mercy of our Lord Jesus Christ unto eternal life. And of some having compassion, making a difference: And others save with fear, pulling them out of the fire; hating even the garment spotted by the flesh. I started to grow in knowledge and God equipped me, my soul strengthened in His spirit as did my clarity in vision.

Ron invited me to come to Saint Paul's House; a mission in NYC. When I attended Times Square church Ron was someone who liked to complain. So he said, "All is not right at the mission. They're serving us stale food while they, the staff, keep the good food for themselves," so I came along to see what God would have me do. I sat at a large oval table and after the pastor said grace he passed the food around. Suddenly the lady who sat next to me caught my eye. After seeing the expression on her face I was moved with compassion and asked her what was wrong. She told me she had an incurable liver disease and she was going to die soon. My reply, "Let us see what the Lord will do." I laid my hand on her liver and quietly said, "In the name of the Lord Jesus Christ be healed." A wave passed as though

203

through my body I felt her need being met as she said, "I feel heat in my body." Then she began to cry but they were tears of joy and the smile on her face told me she was healed (as I remember, later she came to my church and ran into Ron who confirmed it with me. She'd checked with the doctor and, to their surprise, she made a full recovery). I stepped up from the table and found myself in front of a small group of people praying, about a yard from the table. I asked what they were praying about and found out they wanted to receive the Holy Spirit. I joined the circle and instructed them to speak out from their hearts letting their thoughts be still and about several in all received the spirit of the Living God.

Sometime later my wife sent me out for some groceries. Walking into a supermarket I went to cut through a checkout line, passing the person I slipped by. The next person on line was an elderly lady with silver-gray hair. All at once she started to shake all over uncontrollably. It was as if every fiber of her being was crying out for help with nowhere to turn. She turned ashen white and fell over. I caught her kneeling on the floor. I became moved with compassion as she became as my little baby daughter. A wave of love swept through me and into her as I stroked her hair, her peace was restored as she looked up to me with absolute trust in her eyes and asked, "Do I know you?" All at once a spirit hit her. "Oh I'm holding up the line. I've got to get busy. I've so much to do." She started shaking all over again, another wave of love went through me as I caught her in a second. This time she asked me with little girl trusting eyes. "What do I do?" "You've got to be at peace. You're more important than all the business of your life." I told her I was putting something to read in her bag (a bible tract with a plan of salvation) and to read it when she got home. She arose with rosy red cheeks with a look of complete peace. Then some paramedics arrived and started to question her. I slipped away never to see this Jewish lady named Mosha again, after one last glance to see her beaming from ear to ear with a smile a mile long as the paramedics questioned her.

All at once I was interrupted by another woman shouting, "You breathed life into her. I saw you breathe life into that lady." I told her I followed the teachings of Jesus and to start reading first the book of Ecclesiastes in the old testament. I assured her God would instruct her with His word, then pushed my cart and started with my grocery shopping, shaking excitedly with joy.

The Lord showed me my walk was not always stable, and although He's used me in spite of myself, Jesus has lead me to be still and has healed me as well. As the sun does shine in the sky, the earth orbits around the sun and the moon around the earth, there are absolutes that sustain life; there is order. In my youth how foolish it was to take things that suggested order for granted. They were all there telling me I had an absolute plan for my life, and that I was living out of order.

I never had a mentor or ever would take advice, integrity was non-existent with me. Drugs, writing graffiti and sex were all acting out rebellious lifestyles for me, for I was never shown or made to feel safe in an orderly one. I was a coward running away from my responsibilities, serving my fears, till I met God.

Lord I thank you for bringing order into my life through the character of your son, Jesus. I know now that you're a God of order and as I trust your plan I no longer will have to act out but have peace restored to my life as I follow your ways.

I don't go seeking miracles, I seek Jesus and whatever He brings my way is fine with me. I rejoice more that my name is written in the lambs book of life. I've found walking with Jesus each day is a miracle and I'm always excited to find what every new day will bring, as I walk following the King.

I have taken God at His word and mixed His thoughts with my thoughts. His love is shaping me, through the adversity of the lie of out-of-order orderliness, which tries to block the way of the eternal flame to be sewn within the fibers of my being. It is my desire to have hold of Christ with a focal point that cuts through time continually. As fuel, the more I read my bible and pray, the brighter the flame burns still, opening wider the door to eternity which keeps all darkened thoughts away; showing me the way to go for life, the more I share of it the more I receive too and possess this eternal land with peace forevermore.

I see Eternity as a pinhole in my eye through a door which leads far from here and into there.

I feel your peace my Lord and I know that you are with me.

Though life may seem a struggle at times you burn in me and I remember to call, call out to you and you burn brighter still.

I call till you outshine the sun

Then all my problems get so small, then not at all.

The reality of this world is cold, tries to build its ice frozen to enter in to our relationship with Christ to put out the fire of eternal light,with its hollow residue.

It is a lie which tells us to fear and we march the wrong way landing to camp out in the mouth which jaws are hell never realizing the darkness of the way until they close.

A fresh dose of God's word will pierce the veil causing us to stay consciously aware manna from on high will fall as we admire the changes, the stages of a growing plant, how much more are we to enjoy and love the crown of creation of the fragrance of eternal life in man.

I see a frightened child, then I see many calling out of the darkness of the night with no answers in their sight to hide their naked pain.

A front is put up, a fence to keep people away to hide their fears of being discovered.

With everything stripped away worthless, then who are they?

We need to be joined to the love of God, a conscience remembrance, to be.

When we fear we try to hold on for security to a claim we have an identity all of our own and must take, to make it bigger feel safer still building on an insecure base for we don't know who we are, too scared to face it and don't admit it for now a lie has become our truth.

Till we trust to connect with love from God a new reality awaits if we want to be pulled from the pit.

People trying to protect themselves so sad.

When to look onto God who cares to protect us as we look on.

Or do we just stare, tired of fright, or just numb to who cares, Please remember this in your fears.

God loves us enough to spend time with us each and every day, in every way.

So we won't have to be afraid anymore.

About the Author

Disillusioned with life I got off the ride to see what kind of animal I was riding. It was a beast with promises of pleasure with no satisfaction. There had to be something better than this, my search had become a reality orientated one. Where there'd be no stopping till I'd find where it would link up with satisfaction.

After my search I found a living God who both satisifes and brings order in the midst of a confused world. My life is about remaining joined through relating to God's sanity through Jesus Christ. I meditate upon God's word, I call out to Him and I am restored.

I'm not ashamed of the power of Jesus Christ, I've been touched by His great love. I've been changed through Gods forgiveness. I'm no longer the insane man I used to be. Now I'm sensitive to those who seek freedom from the hatered of what they've become and don't know where to turn. The way I once did till I found Christ. Don't know me, know Jesus in me. That we may be brothers and sisters in a rather large family. I lay down my life for others, the way Jesus did for me, that others may see His light in me and go free also.